Marriage in a Nutshell
Expanded Edition

Marriage in a Nutshell
Expanded Edition

Proverbs and Commentaries
About Marriage Selected From
The Biblical Book of Proverbs
And Other Sources

Now Including Additional Commentary,
Study Activities,
And Discussion Questions for Couples
And Small Groups

Robert A. Harris

.:Virtual**Salt**®
Publishing
Tustin

Marriage in a Nutshell
Expanded Edition

Proverbs and Commentaries about Marriage
Selected from the Biblical Book of Proverbs
and Other Sources

Now Including Additional Commentary,
Study Activities and Discussion Questions for
Couples And Small Groups

VirtualSalt® Publishing, Tustin, California
© 2020, 2014 Robert A. Harris
All rights reserved

ISBN 978-1-941233-25-2 [Paperback]
ISBN 978-1-941233-26-9 [eBook]

www.virtualsalt.com

VirtualSalt® is a registered trademark of
Robert Alan Harris

Except where noted, Scripture translations are from the New American Standard Bible (NASB), © 1971 The Lockman Foundation.

cc

Introduction

*Ask not what your marriage can do for you;
Ask what you can do for your marriage.*

My interest in marriage and relationships started many years ago, while I was still single, observing married couples interact. I saw some couples function as a harmonious unit getting enormous fun out of marriage; and I saw other couples treating each other as enemies and getting only bitterness out of marriage. In later years, my continued observation, personal experience, and substantial research led me to consider sharing what I had learned. I began mounting articles on my Web site about improving relationships.

Then one day I witnessed a young couple in a supermarket arguing in hostile tones over whether to buy a particular jar of jelly. I thought, "What are they thinking? Two people supposedly joined in the bonds of the most joyful, satisfying, friendship possible, destroying their happiness over a three-dollar jar of jelly — which was probably made with high-fructose corn syrup instead of real sugar anyway." I thought further, "If only they knew that there is a way to find happiness and fulfillment in marriage."

I knew that marriage is a complex topic, and that there were many lengthy books about it. I also knew that what busy couples might benefit from most today would be a short, direct, practical treatment. In other words, *Marriage in a Nutshell*.[1] Not long after that, I was reading in the Biblical book of Proverbs, and the idea for the current volume took root. Connect the principles of marital harmony with the Biblical wisdom of Proverbs, proved over thousands of years, and the result would be a short, practical, and effective discussion about avoiding (or remedying) marital discontent.

The first edition of the book matched its name well: It was fewer than 100 pages, presenting the practical, psychological, sociological, emotional, and intellectual elements needed to produce a harmonious marriage.

Expanded Edition

The original edition of *Marriage in a Nutshell* was, indeed, a small book. But soon it began to be used as a weekly text for Sunday School, and study notes and other materials were produced to support the little book for group study. These supports are now included in this much larger Expanded Edition, with over 270 pages.

Readers who still want the original shorter version will be happy to note that it is still here, presented in the first part of each chapter, before the Discussion Questions.

---

[1] The old expression, "an Iliad in nutshell," referred to a long work such as Homer's Iliad being condensed enough that it fit into a walnut shell. Thus, Marriage in a Nutshell seemed to be an appropriate title for the less-than-a-hundred-page book.

New for the Expanded Edition are:
- Discussion Questions for each proverb for exploring the theme and sharing input by participants
- Quotations for Discussion with comments by well-respected writers
- Important Scriptures that relate to the theme of each proverb
- Additional Commentary further laying out the topic
- Word Studies exploring some of the significant Greek and Hebrew words
- Five Secret Keys to a Happy Marriage
- The Five Cruel Truths about Marriage for Brides
- The Ten Commandments of Marriage
- You Be the Counselor activities that allow participants to turn the tables and offer (rather than just receive) advice
- A Prayer related to each proverb
- Educational posters emphasizing important themes and concepts

Ideally, readers should make this book an active, interaction guide, helping them grow in faith, maturity, and interpersonal skills.

Now, thanks to my best friend, inspiration, and excellent wife (Proverbs 31:10), Marie, for her encouragement with this project.

Tustin, February, 2020

Part One
Biblical Proverbs

1

Do not let kindness and truth leave you;
Bind them around your neck,
Write them on the tablet of your heart,
So you will find favor and good repute
In the sight of God and man.
—Proverbs 3:3-4

It might seem like a strange pair, but two critically important characteristics for building and maintaining a relationship are kindness and truth.

Kindness can be a few words of appreciation, love, or support, or it can be a simple caress, a note, a backrub, or even a small gift. It's the emotional accompaniment to whatever you say or do that is important.

We are trained by our culture to look for defects and failures; therefore, we neither give nor get the soft and gentle words and actions that bring music to our souls at midnight (to paraphrase 17th century poet George Herbert). The kindness of a sympathetic smile can do wonders for encouraging a spouse (or friend) in this all-too-frequently hostile life.

Truth means honesty in the relationship. It doesn't mean criticizing your spouse in the name of truth ("You seem to be gaining a lot of weight; better lay off those chocolates"). It does mean admitting that you lost the TV remote or that you give an honest answer when asked if you enjoy, say, going fishing.

Marriage relationships are built up (or torn apart) a little at a time. The building blocks of marriage are made of trust, commitment, loyalty, sharing, working together, love, respect, honesty, and many more.

But the mortar that holds all these blocks together is made from a mixture of kindness and truth.

✠ ◆ ✠

Discussion Questions
1. Why is kindness an important characteristic for *building* a relationship?
2. Why is kindness important for *maintaining* a relationship?
3. Why is truth and an "honest answer" important?
4. What about telling "little white lies" to keep someone happy?
5. Complete the sentence. *"If you want your partner always to be truthful with you, then you . . ."*
6. Think about the matching of kindness with truth. What relationship can you discern? Tell the truth with kindness? Be kind truthfully? (That is, don't praise your spouse for a quality that he or she does not have.)

> **The Voice of Experience**
> Recently, a 90-year-old widow was asked, "What was the most important and the most powerful lesson you have learned about making a marriage successful?"
> The widow answered, **"Always tell the truth."**

Quotation for Discussion
"A committed relationship is a contract of mutual trust, respect, nurturance, and protection. *Anything* that violates that contract can become traitorous."
—John Gottman, *What Makes Love Last?*, page 66

You Be the Counselor
1. What advice would you give a person who was always cold and abrupt with his or her spouse?
2. How does being "loose with the truth" impair a relationship? What would you say to someone who has a problem like this?
3. Do you know anyone whose marriage was not deeply committed to kindness and truth? If so, why, do you think, that is or was the case? What happened to that relationship?

Scripture
"No one who practices deceit shall dwell in my house; no one who utters lies shall continue before my eyes."
—Psalm 101:7 (ESV)

Additional Commentary
In the greatest commandment, we are told to love God with both heart and mind, the emotions and the intellect. In the proverb, kindness represents the emotional aspect of our love for God—and for our neighbor—and for our spouse—while truth represents the intellectual aspect.

What does it mean to say that "the emotional accompaniment . . . is important"? A waitress (or spouse!) can plop a cup of coffee in front of you without saying a word. Or she can make eye contact and say warmly, "Here's your coffee. It's a fresh batch. Enjoy it." The first instance represents an act. The second represents a kind act. The formula is easy:

> An Act + Kindness = A Kind Act.

The emotional accompaniment to our actions makes them kind or not. The value in the act is the degree of kindness transmitted by the actor and the degree perceived by the recipient. An action without kindness can be hurtful. Suppose a husband walks into the house and says to his wife:

> *Husband 1: "Well, I missed half of the most important game of the season, but I got your car washed. I hope you're satisfied."*

Here the husband has performed an act, but he has not performed a kind act. Instead, he has used the act as an emotional weapon, hoping to shame his wife and have her feel guilt. Compare:

> *Husband 2: "Your car is now looking like new, Sweetie. After I washed it, I polished it really well with that special SuperGlint car wax."*

Note also that kind words in response can form a kind act. Suppose the wife of Husband 2 says:

> *Wife 2: "Thank you so much, darling. I really appreciate your help. And I'm sorry you had to miss half the game. You didn't have to do that, you know. But thanks again. It looks nice."*

On the other hand, a hostile response to a kind act becomes a rejection of the attempt at kindness or closeness. Suppose the wife of Husband 2 had replied to his comment with this:

> *Wife 1: "Well, thanks, I suppose, for washing the car, as you call it. I see you were in a rush to get to the game and missed several spots. I'll just take it to the car wash tomorrow where they will do it right."*

Such a comment easily turns a joy into a pain and goes one step further toward refrigerating the relationship.

Secret Key #1 to a Happy Marriage
Never use a negative or sarcastic tone of voice.

Word Study
The word for *kindness* in the Hebrew is *checed*, meaning kindness, favor, goodness, abundant in kindness (Strong's 2617). Look up other Scriptures where this word appears and discuss.

The word for *truth* in the Hebrew is *emeth*, meaning truth, firmness, faithfulness, reliability, sureness, stability (Strong's 571). Look up other Scriptures where this word appears and discuss.

My Takeaway
Think about what you have learned. What is the most important thing you will take from this chapter? What is your "action item"?

✠
✠ ✠

PRAYER
LORD, as I work through my day and encounter many challenges, often in the form of other people, help me always to remember that they live and act according to the light you have given them. May I treat each person with kindness and compassion,

regardless of how they treat me. And may your truth be my standard and guide in every situation. I ask this and I thank you in the name of Jesus my Savior. Amen.

✝

2

Drink water from your own cistern,
And fresh water from your own well.
And rejoice in the wife of your youth.
—Proverbs 5:15, 18a

Be faithful to your own wife and don't commit adultery (drinking water from your neighbor's cistern). And don't just put up with, don't just endure, don't just live with, but rejoice in your wife. If that seems difficult or impossible, then you need to work on your relationship. Spend time together, talking, making something, serving others.

It has been known since the days of Aristotle that if you act in a certain way, your beliefs and feelings will eventually harmonize with those actions. So, if you are feeling cold or bored or frustrated with your spouse, act as if you were feeling warm, interested, and happy with your spouse. You will be surprised at the difference. And your spouse just might change, too, since changing yourself is always the first step toward getting an improved spouse.

✠ ◆ ✠

Discussion Questions
1. What causes relationships to stagnate and grow boring?

2. Marriage experts say that a spouse who starts to think about drinking water from the neighbor's cistern does so because of feeling lonely and disconnected from their partner. What are some ways to maintain emotional connection with a spouse?
3. What is one specific thing a husband can do to move from "just living with" his wife to "rejoicing in his wife"?
4. Marriage counselors often give the advice here, for cold, uninterested, unhappy spouses to act as if they felt warm, interested, and happy with their partner. Do you know of anyone who has used this approach toward changing behavior?
5. What does the commentary mean when it says that "changing yourself is always the first step toward an improved spouse"?

Quotation for Discussion
"Most affairs are not about sex. They are about coping with a lonely marriage by finding someone interested in you."
—John Gottman, *What Makes Love Last*, page 60

Scripture
"Husbands, love your wives, just as Christ also loved the church and gave himself up for her. . . . So husbands ought also to love their own wives as their own bodies. He who loves his own wife loves himself. . . ."
—Ephesians 5:25, 28 (NASB)

You Be the Counselor
1. What advice would you give to a couple (spouses or friends) who felt that they had grown apart and were no longer "rejoicing" in each other?
2. Would you advise those spouses who feel cold toward the other one to "fake it till you make

it" and act as if they felt warm and cozy with the other?

Additional Commentary

The advice to act as if you are feeling warm and friendly in order to make yourself and your spouse warm and friendly has more than the backing of Aristotle. We are all highly influenced by our environment and by what we see others doing and feeling. People tend to mimic the facial expressions and arm positions of those they are talking to. Little kids ask, "Are we having fun?" And of course, if you think some sitcom is funny, it might be largely because of the recorded laugh track added to it, designed to influence your response to the jokes.

And if you know a husband whose boredom is preventing him from rejoicing in the wife of his youth, paraphrase Forrest Gump to him, "Boredom is as boredom does." (Who, exactly, is in charge of the excitement schedule in a marriage?)

The Krazy Kounselor Speaks

The people asked the Krazy Kounselor, "Why do some men seem to love their cars more than they love their wives?"

The Krazy Kounselor answered, "Many men spend more time focusing on their cars—washing, polishing, wiping—than the time they spend with their wives. These men are intentional about concentrating on their cars, focusing on them as they wash them. Time spent with something increases enjoyment."

Then the people said, "Your comment makes no sense. Most men these days just take their car to the car wash. And even if they did wash their own cars, how could that information be used to improve a marriage?"

The Krazy Kounselor replied, "The husband should wash his wife. Get a bucket of warm, sudsy water and a very soft sponge. Use the sponge to wash your wife down from neck to toes, paying attention as you gently move the sponge over the curves of her body. Then rinse and pat dry."

"That's crazy," the people said.

My Takeaway
Think about what you have learned. What is the most important thing you will take from this chapter? What is your "action item"?

☦
☦ ☦

Prayer

LORD, we thank you for bringing us together as husband and wife, and pray that we will live out your plan for our lives and our marriage. Keep us ever committed to you and to each other, living always confident in our love. And if conflicts should arise, may we always keep in mind that we are partners together, working toward the single goal of serving you. In Jesus' name we pray. Amen.

☦

3
*Hatred stirs up strife,
But love covers all transgressions.*
—Proverbs 10:12

Exchanging negative, critical, and unloving comments only perpetuates the strife and tension and coldness in a marriage. Showing real love, consideration, understanding, forgiveness, and kindness will wash away the faults and hurts. It's a choice. Which behavior do you think will make your spouse happier? Which do you think will make you happier?

Love, real love, has a strange way of covering transgressions. First, the saying, "Love is blind," means that in a marriage partnership, spouses simply don't see the "transgressions" that other people see. To use our standard example, a loving partner who sees the cap missing from the toothpaste tube simply doesn't see that fact as a transgression on the spouse's part. The partner simply puts the cap back on and moves on to the mouthwash or whatever is the next item on the day's agenda.

Second, the spouse might recognize a failing in the partner, but just doesn't care. In the context of the relationship, the spouse allows the partner to be human and to possess individual quirks.

Andrea: Why, Paula, I never saw such a germophobic man as your husband. He even washes the doorknobs.
Paula: Yeah, he keeps things clean all right.
Andrea: Doesn't that bug you?
Paula: Not at all. I know it might seem a bit excessive, but on the other hand, we've not had colds for three years.

Third, the spouse might be bothered by the partner's behavior, but simply accepts it out of love and doesn't say anything.

Bill: Hey, Sid. I've noticed that your wife interrupts you and talks over you.
Sid: Yeah, she does.
Bill: Doesn't that bother you? I'd be fuming.
Sid: It bothers me some, sure. But I've decided not to say anything.
Bill: Why ever not?
Sid: It's a long-standing habit, and I doubt she could change. And besides, it's too minor a thing to bring up right now.

✠ ◆ ✠

Discussion Questions
1. When people argue, what usually happens to the emotions of both?
2. Explain the saying, "Always discuss; never argue."
3. How does Paul's description of love in 1 Corinthians 13:4-8 support this proverb? See the Love poster on the next page.

Love

                              is patient
              is kind
                              does not envy
        does not boast
                              is not arrogant
              is not rude
                              does not insist on its own way
              is not irritable
                              is not resentful
    does not rejoice at wrongdoing
                              rejoices with the truth
              bears all things
                              believes all things
              hopes all things
                              endures all things

Love Never Ends

4. Discuss the differences between Love and Hatred. Does hatred derive from a focus on the self?

Hatred

                              is impatient
              is unkind
                              envies
              boasts
                              is arrogant
              is rude
                              insists on its own way
              is irritable
                              is resentful
        rejoices at wrongdoing
                              rejoices with falsehood
              bears nothing
                              believes nothing
              hopes for nothing
                              endures nothing

Hatred Ends

5. Locate half a dozen different translations of the Bible and compare each one's version of 1 Corinthians 13:4-8. How do the variations enhance your understanding of Biblical teaching about love?

Quotations for Discussion

"There is no such thing as constructive criticism. . . . Criticism triggers defensiveness, which prevents resolution of an argument." —John Gottman, *What Makes Love Last?*, page 120

"But there's a world of difference between a complaint and a criticism. A complaint only addresses the specific action at which your spouse failed. A criticism is more global—it adds on some negative words about your mate's character or personality." —John Gottman, *The Seven Principles for Making Marriage Work*, page 27

You Be the Counselor

Counsel this couple:

> Bing: *You forgot to put away your deodorant again.*
>
> Bong: *That's because I was busy cleaning the sink that you left so dirty.*
>
> Bing: *I didn't have time because I was late after spending twenty minutes hunting for the toothpaste, which you always hide.*
>
> Bong: *You should talk. I swear, I can never find the stamps once you've been writing to Sam.*
>
> Bing: *I haven't written to Sam in weeks. But you misplace the shed keys every day.*
>
> Bong: *No, you just think the shed keys belong in that junk bowl on the counter. I always put them right where they belong. You're the one who keeps misplacing them.*
>
> Bing: *You never go into the shed, anyway. So why should the keys go on that ugly key rack*

> *you put in an almost inaccessible place instead of the easy-to-reach bowl near the door?*
>
> *Bong: So you want our house and lives to be buried in miscellaneous junk just to suit your convenience.*

My Takeaway

Think about what you have learned. What is the most important thing you will take from this chapter? What is your "action item"?

✠
✠ ✠
Prayer

Dear LORD, we are so deeply grateful that you have chosen to love us rather than hate us, even though we are too often rebellious and disobedient. Please help us to govern our own tempers and behaviors so that we can show love rather than hatred toward those who irritate or even wrong us. May we grow in patience, graciousness, and gentleness towards everyone, especially the members of our own household. And may you rule in our hearts and actions always. In Jesus' name. Amen.

✞

4
A gracious woman attains honor.
—Proverbs 11:16a

Yes, the gracious—the kind, pleasant, amiable—woman is just more fun to be around, and gains the high reputation she deserves. She is honored for her easygoing personality, and her willingness to jump in and help cheerfully.

Maybe this is the place to mention that Secret Key #2 to a Happy Marriage is to focus your relational energies, choices, habits, practices—and words—on making life for your spouse easier rather than more difficult.

Secret Key #2 to a Happy Marriage
Make your every word and deed focus on making life for your spouse easier rather than more difficult.

That's why, when coming home from work and turning the corner onto his street, the husband of a gracious wife starts to relax and to become aware of a feeling of comfort and anticipation rising in his heart. As he pulls into his driveway, he says to himself, "Ah, home at last to my sanctuary and my loving wife, the delight of my life."

✠ ◆ ✠

Discussion Questions
1. How would you define "gracious"?
2. What is a sanctuary? (Look up the Biblical concept of sanctuary cities if you need help.)
3. What makes a home a sanctuary?
4. What appeals to you about the Sanctuary poster?
5. Does the Sanctuary poster present some ideals that you would like your home to have? Choose one and explain in a sentence or two why you would like to adopt it.
6. Would you consider putting the poster up in your house? Why or Why not?

Sanctuary Poster

Think about this poster and how it can and should shape the behavior of those who live in the home where it is posted.

> This is More Than a House.
> **This is a Home.**
> **A Sanctuary.**
> This is a Place of
> **Refuge,**
> **Safety, and**
> **Peace.**
> **Here Grace Overcomes**
> Criticism,
> Competition, and
> Conflict.
> Here You Can Expect
> **Comfort,**
> **Care, and**
> **Compassion.**

Quotation for Discussion
"Safety is honor in action. Safe people focus on loving the other person rather than measuring how much they are being loved." —Greg Smalley, in *The Best Advice I Ever Got on Marriage*, page xi

Scripture
"And God is able to make all grace abound to you, so that always having all sufficiency in everything, you may have an abundance for every good deed."
—2 Corinthians 9:8

You Be the Counselor
1. How would you share the Secret Key #2 to a Happy Marriage with a young, recently married couple—who needed it?
2. Based on your own marriage or relationships, how would you counsel yourselves using the Secret Key #2?
3. Have you observed the Secret Key #2 working or not working in marriage relationships?
4. How would you use the Sanctuary poster as an aid in counseling?

Additional Commentary
An example of graciousness comes from Lea Salonga, the singing voice of Princess Jasmine in Disney's cartoon, *Aladdin*. Since "A Whole New World" has become her signature song, she sings it at concerts. But it's a duet. Often, she chooses an audience member to sing the male part.

Word Study
Grace, gracious, and *graciousness* represent a key attribute in God's dealing with us and with our dealing with each other.
1. To explore this more fully, use Bible software or go online and find all the references to *grace,*

gracious, and *graciousness*. What can you conclude from these verses?
2. Use Strong's concordance (online or print) to look up the original Hebrew and Greek words translated *grace* in the Bible. Hebrew: Strong's H2580; Greek: Strong's G5485. What can you conclude from this study?

My Takeaway

Think about what you have learned. What is the most important thing you will take from this chapter? What is your "action item"?

✠
✠ ✠
Prayer

LORD, we simply cannot adequately express our gratitude for your unceasing and extravagant grace in our lives. The kind encouragement and love and support you give us in your word provide the confidence we need to rejoice in our relationship with you regardless of our current circumstances. May each of us adopt and live out in our marriage this model of love you have given us, by providing encouragement, kindness, and support for our spouse. And by these words and deeds, may our spouse see you in us. In Jesus' name. Amen.

✞

5
As a ring of gold in a swine's snout,
So is a beautiful woman who lacks discretion.
—Proverbs 11:22

The point of this proverb is to remind us that discretion—being careful and considerate in one's speech and actions—is more important than looks for a lastingly happy marriage. True, gorgeous women who are wise and circumspect are wonderful, but discretion, like amiability and compassion and good sense, makes a woman attractive in a way that even very good looks by themselves just can't match.

This proverb also reminds wives not to gossip, especially about their husbands.

✠ ♦ ✠

Discussion Questions
1. Why is a lack of discretion in someone so problematic for that person's friends or spouse?
2. How do the characteristics of discretion contribute to a healthier relationship?
3. Why do you think gossip is mentioned in the discussion of a proverb about discretion?

Quotation for Discussion
"Generally, it isn't the large bombs of life that do the most damage; it's the gnawing away of serenity

and good sense by pettiness that is the most destructive force of intimate relationships in general, and men-women relationships most specifically."
—Dr. Laura Schlessinger, *Ten Stupid Things Couples Do to Mess Up Their Relationships,* page 75

Scripture for Reflection and Discussion
"Let no unwholesome word proceed from your mouth, but only such a word as is good for edification according to the need of the moment, so that it will give grace to those who hear."
—Ephesians 4:29

Discretion Poster
1. Explain how each of the words in the poster help to define *discretion* in a marriage or other relationship.
2. Which idea or behavior is the most important to have as a discreet person? Why?

Discerning
cons**I**derate
compa**S**sionate
Careful
delibe**R**ative
wis**E**
Thoughtful
c**I**rcumspect
judici**O**us
prude**N**t

You Be the Counselor
At work, Jane frequently talks with several coworkers at lunch about the details of her marriage to her husband Tom, including every argument. At a company party, Tom got stares and glares and smirks from several of Jane's coworkers.

> Tom: "I was horrified, embarrassed, and humiliated by what Jane told her friends."
>
> Jane: "It's just normal girl talk. Besides, they aren't my friends. They are just coworkers."

How would you counsel Tom and Jane?

Word Study
Discretion = Hebrew *taam*, (Strong's 2940). Definition: taste, judgment, discernment, discretion. Find cross-references to this word elsewhere in the Bible, or find several other Bible versions and see how they translate the word in Proverbs 11:22.

My Takeaway
Think about what you have learned. What is the most important thing you will take from this chapter? What is your "action item"?

✠
✠ ✠
PRAYER

Dear LORD, we thank you for giving us life and purpose, and for forgiving us when our tongues slip. Help us to resist the influence of the world, that wants us to blurt out our every thought and private story. Give us the strength to maintain confidences within our relationships and to avoid gossip of every kind. May we shine as models of discretion. In Jesus' name we thank you. Amen.

✠

6
An excellent wife is the crown of her husband,
But she who shames him
Is as rottenness to his bones.
—Proverbs 12:4

An excellent wife makes her husband so happy that he feels like a king. Of all the possessions, talents, friends, and power he may have, his excellent wife is his crown, his glory that establishes his heart in joy. She is the earthly relationship that empowers him and makes him feel like royalty.

And since, as the saying is, the corruption of the best of things creates the worst of things, so is a wife who brings shame on her husband. Having rotten bones isn't a good thing; feeling *as if* you have rotten bones can't be much better.

✠ ◆ ✠

Discussion Questions
1. Give some scenarios and comments that would be examples of a wife being the crown of her husband.
2. Why do you think this proverb was important enough to include in the Bible and in this book?
3. Give some scenarios and comments that would be examples of a wife shaming her husband.

4. Are men hurt more by being shamed than women? Discuss.
5. What are some things that would be the opposite of shame? (Hint: Google "shame antonyms.")

Scripture
"Do nothing from selfishness or empty conceit, but with humility of mind regard one another as more important than yourselves; do not merely look out for your own personal interests, but also for the interests of others." —Philippians 2:3-4

Word Study
Excellent = Hebrew *chayil*. Definition: army, strength, efficiency, wealth, valor, virtue, ability often involving moral worth

Shame = Hebrew *bosh*. Definition: be ashamed, causing shame, bringing shame on

1. The word translated *excellent* in this passage has several meanings. Which one do you think would be the best in this proverb? Why?
2. Does learning the meanings of the Hebrew for *excellent* alter your understanding of this proverb and what constitutes an "excellent" wife?

The Krazy Kounselor Speaks
The people asked, "How can a wife make her husband feel like a king?"

The Krazy Kounselor answered, "In our society, both men and women receive much more criticism than praise. And for some reason, in many cases, wives are much more critical of their husbands than husbands are of their wives."

"Your mind is wandering, O Krazy one," the people said. "You can't seem to pay attention or focus. We asked you about making a husband feel like a king."

"Have the wife cut a piece of paper into ten parts. On each part, she should write down a compliment about her husband. Something she likes about him."

"Let's hope she can find ten things," the people said, sarcastically.

"Then," concluded the Krazy Kounselor, "when she has a criticism she wants to deliver, let her first deliver each of the ten compliments, discussing each and reinforcing them, and putting them up somewhere. Finally, she can deliver her complaint."

"That's crazy," the people said.

"Husbands who are reflexively critical of their wives should follow the same practice."

My Takeaway

Think about what you have learned. What is the most important thing you will take from this chapter? What is your "action item"?

☘
☘ ☘

Prayer

Dear LORD, you have been so gracious and merciful as to take away the deep shame of our sins. Without your kindness, we would be truly wretched creatures, hiding our faces from you. Help us, then, to refrain from using shame to punish our loved ones, and instead to encourage them along the path of righteousness. We praise you and thank you in Jesus' name. Amen.

☘

7
There is one who speaks rashly
Like the thrusts of a sword,
But the tongue of the wise brings healing.
—Proverbs 12:18

Too many people do not realize what a powerful instrument the tongue is. A harsh word can do a lot of damage, while a kind word can heal deep hurts.

The saying, "Sticks and stones will break my bones, but words can never hurt me," is false. The truth is, "A stick hurts for an hour, but words can hurt for years."

"Think before you speak" has become almost a cliché, but there is good reason for it. Unfortunately, this advice is sometimes ignored.

When you are tempted to say something critical to your spouse, especially if you are going to add a harsh tone of voice, first ask yourself, "What do I expect the result to be? Will my comment make my spouse happier? If not, why should I say it? Or do I think it will make me happier? Do I really think that making my spouse unhappy will make me happy?"

And if you fire a verbal salvo at your spouse, what will your spouse do? Do you think the next ten minutes will be a time of strengthening your relationship and increasing your marital satisfaction?

It is unfortunate that when some spouses disagree, one spouse or both will make comments intended to hurt the other one. This use of words as punishment is what some parents do with their children, when the parent wants the child to know "how much his actions bother me."

Important Reminder: Your spouse is not your child. Don't treat your life partner the way you treat your kids. It's condescending and humiliating and devaluing. So just stop it.

> **Secret Key #3 to a Happy Marriage**
> Always Remember Respect.
> Avoid sarcasm, insults, and condescension.

And, of course, you shouldn't treat your kids this way, either. Verbal beatings are very harmful to children as well as adults.

Use your tongue to soothe and heal, not to stab and cut.

✠ ◆ ✠

Discussion Questions
1. What are some ways that "one who speaks rashly" can cause cuts like "the thrusts of a sword"?
2. How can the tongue bring healing? Give some examples of healing words.
3. Why is it the tongue of "the wise" that brings healing? How does wisdom fit in here?
4. "Think before you speak" is good advice. How can it be followed more completely, especially during an animated discussion?

Quotation for Discussion
"With our words we either beat the life out of our marriage or we cultivate, feed, and water it to ensure happy years ahead." —Joni Eareckson Tada, "The Art of Affirmation."

Additional Commentary
"Simple conversation" isn't so simple. Communication is a complex phenomenon. The received meaning of a speaker's message (or comment) is a product of
- the speaker's words
- the speaker's tone of voice
- the speaker's physical presentation when in person (facial expression, gestures, posture)
- the receiver's expectations
- the receiver's understanding of the meaning of the speaker's words
    - The denotation or dictionary definition (what the receiver assumes is the dictionary definition)
    - The connotation or emotional meaning that the receiver attaches to the words
- the general context of the two people's broad relationship—that is, how they usually interact, what they usually mean, what the emotional overtones usually are.

It shouldn't be surprising, then, to realize that the speaker's intended communication and the receiver's received meaning can be quite different.

Tone of Voice Activity
Choose one or more of the following phrases and say them in each tone of voice. Feel free to add facial expressions as appropriate.

Discuss the differences in received meaning each version is likely to produce.

Word or Phrase	Tone of Voice
Thank you so much	Polite but cool
I'm really sorry	Sincere
I love you, too	Sarcastic
I was wrong	Flat and fast
Excuse me	Drawn out
You're right	Insincere

My Takeaway

Think about what you have learned. What is the most important thing you will take from this chapter? What is your "action item"?

✠
✠ ✠

Prayer

Lord, we thank you so very much for the ability you have given us to speak. Speaking is a blessing we too often take for granted. And we sometimes let our speech get ahead of our thoughts. Please, Lord, help us to remember the power of speech and how much harm even a few careless words can do. Prevent us, we pray, from weaponizing our speech, and instead, let our words be kind and helpful and healing. And help us to remember how much good even a few encouraging words can do. We ask in the name of the Word of God, Jesus. Amen.

✟

8

The wise woman builds her house,
But the foolish tears it down
With her own hands.
—Proverbs 14:1

Marriage is a house you build together with your spouse. The wise woman builds her house by building up her husband. Words of appreciation and support toward her husband help him grow stronger and more confident—and more loving toward his wife. The foolish woman uses criticism and complaint and lecturing to punish her husband. Emotionally destructive words tear him down and the house is torn apart.

Marriages succeed and are continuously built up through kindness and compassion, or they fail by being constantly torn apart through bickering and disapproval—by either spouse, or both.

External threats and attacks can be repelled by a strong marriage partnership, heavily influenced by the wisdom of the wife; but internal strife can be fatal, especially when the partners act foolishly and inconsiderately.

Before you engage in the next altercation, stop and ask yourself, "Why am I planning to use these words, these details, and this tone of voice? Am I confident that they will make my spouse happier and my marriage stronger? Or will they rip out yet another supporting beam, one less to hold the roof up?"

Note finally, this proverb focuses on the wise and foolish women because women wield the greater emotional power in a marriage. Men deeply need respect, approval, and encouragement, and the wives who provide that build their houses on solid ground. And in such a house dwells a husband's love.

Discussion Questions
1. Why, do you think, the foolish woman acts foolishly? She must want happiness as much as the wise woman.
2. What are some ways the wise woman can build her house, besides those mentioned in the book?
3. What does the concept of "marriage partnership" mean to you? How is it connected to the metaphor of building a house?

Quotation for Discussion
"Many women feel that the only way they can get what they need in a relationship is to criticize a man when he makes mistakes and to offer unsolicited advice" (page 78). But, "A man's deepest fear is that he is not good enough or that he is incompetent" (page 56). And, "men are sensitive to feeling that they have failed when a woman talks about problems. This is why it is so hard for him to listen sometimes. He wants to be her hero. When she is disappointed or unhappy over anything, he feels like a failure. Her unhappiness confirms his deep-

est fear: he is just not good enough. Many women today don't realize how vulnerable men are and how much they need love, too" (pages 57-58).

—John Gray, *Men Are from Mars, Women Are from Venus*.

Scripture
"So then, we must pursue what promotes peace and what builds up one another." —Romans 14:19 (HCSB)

Wielding the Hammer To Build or To Tear Down
Use this table to answer the questions that follow.

Wielding the Hammer To Build or To Tear Down	
Building Words	**Tearing Down Words**
Appreciating, Grateful	Criticizing
Encouraging	Discouraging
Supportive	Contradicting
Approving, Affirming	Disapproving
Respectful, Honoring	Disrespectful
Kind	Sarcastic
Compassionate	Blaming
Empathetic	Demeaning, Belittling
Understanding	Contentious
Complimenting	Contemptuous

1. How would you counsel a couple if the husband complains that his wife uses only Tearing Down words?
2. How would you counsel the couple if the wife responds to the husband's complaint by saying that her husband is "too sensitive," and adds that she has "the right to her own opinion"?

3. How would you counsel a couple if the wife complains that her husband uses only Tearing Down words?
4. How would you counsel the couple if the husband responds by saying that his wife is "too sensitive to mere words"?
5. Suggest and discuss several other words that describe types of building words and tearing down words. Which are especially helpful and which are especially hurtful?

My Takeaway
Think about what you have learned. What is the most important thing you will take from this chapter? What is your "action item"?

✠
✠ ✠
PRAYER

Dear LORD, thank you for showing us a model of a loving relationship in the way you seek always to build us up and affirm us when we accomplish something worthy, and in the way you bring us peace of heart when we have failed and are suffering. Help us to remember that we, too, are called to be Christ-like in our relationships, building up others and encouraging them.

And help us to remember that the marriage relationship requires special, intentional, and active work to create and maintain a family filled with peace and harmony. With the help of your Spirit, may we always choose words that will increase the love, trust, respect, and joy in each other through however many decades it pleases you to let us live. In Jesus' name we pray. Amen.

✠

9
A gentle answer turns away wrath,
But a harsh word stirs up anger.
—Proverbs 15:1

Respond to anger by listening and seeking to understand sympathetically. Letting your spouse vent will enable him or her to feel heard. Lack of push back or resistance will calm your partner down. On the other hand, if you object, contradict, or resist, you will only make the anger worse, because it will appear to your spouse that you are invalidating his or her feelings and issue.

When your spouse lashes out at you in anger, you might be tempted to pick up your verbal weapons and do battle, with the result that the argument will escalate until perhaps the neighbors can hear you shouting. (And will they talk!)

On the other hand, if you respond gently, you might surprise your spouse, and soon calm the waters. A one-sided rant soon makes the arguer feel a bit foolish.

And something that we all know but that many of us seldom practice often enough is the fact that apologies are free. If your spouse lashes out at you, why not gently and warmly and sincerely say you are sorry? If you don't feel that you have done anything wrong, at least say you're sorry that your spouse is upset.

Some people lose their ability to think rationally when they are angry. And raging irrationality is not a pretty sight. If this is you, next time you feel anger welling up against your spouse, stop the discussion, tell your spouse that you need to take a break to calm down, and go on a walk by yourself for a while. Later, when you can discuss the issue calmly, get together again.

Even serious disagreements—no, make that *especially* serious disagreements—ought to be handled respectfully and reasonably.

Here's a thought: Imagine that your dispute is going to be recorded for a reality TV show called "Spousal Spats." The whole argument will be broadcast to the world. Yes, your mom, grandma, the kids, the neighbors, curious strangers by the million—they will all see it. Let that thought guide your interaction.

Discussion Questions
1. Why is it important to "turn away anger"?
2. What does it mean to say that "it takes two to argue"?
3. What difference do the fundamental qualities of the relationship (friendship, values, attitude) make in the way spouses or others argue?
4. Because "apologies are free," why don't people in an argument apologize more often when they realize they have made a mistake or misunderstood or spoken harshly?

Quotation for Discussion
"When a discussion leads off . . . with criticism and/or sarcasm, a form of contempt, it has begun with a 'harsh startup. . . .if your discussion begins with a harsh startup, it will inevitably end on a negative note. . . . A harsh startup simply dooms you to failure" (page 27).
—John Gottman, *Seven Principles for Making Marriage Work*

Free!
Take One!

**I'm sorry.
Forgive me.
It was my fault.
I regret that.
I apologize.**

Remember:
Apologies Are Free.

Scripture
"Let all bitterness and wrath and anger and clamor and slander be put away from you, along with all malice." —Ephesians 4:31

Additional Commentary
Spouses (and others in relationships such as coworkers) who frequently get into angry exchanges are more likely to be helped if they understand the source or cause behind their behavior. Here, for example, are come factors that can produce loud, harsh disputes.

1. **A fight for control.** Hostile interchanges many times include control issues. "I should be the one who gets to make that decision that you made. I am in charge of this marriage."
2. **Proxy battles.** Fighting over the toothpaste cap or the place the razor goes can involve the use of minor things as proxies (substitutes) for larger, unspoken, issues.
3. **Unreleased anger.** If a spouse had a tough day at work battling a coworker, a committee, or the boss, for example, there may be a storehouse of emotional dynamite that the spouse accidentally sets off. It might be nothing personal, but the arrows to the heart feel very real.
4. **Lack of understanding of the other sex.** Spouses who do not understand how different men and women are from each other are often upset when their spouse doesn't do or say what seems obvious to them.

You Be the Counselor
1. How would you counsel a couple whose disagreements turn into shouting matches?
2. How would you counsel a couple whose disagreements end in the couple giving each other the "silent treatment" for a week or more?
3. Which of the following might be an effective way to stop an argument and start working on the problem?
    - Declare a truce for 4, 8, or 24 hours to allow time to cool off and think things through.
    - Each spouse should write down a description of the disagreement or issue and also write down ideas toward a resolution. (This idea helps prevent or reduce the degree of misunderstanding each spouse has.)

- Each spouse should take the other spouse's position and present the reasons, evidence, and arguments their spouse could use.
- The spouses should work together to define the terms of the dispute as specifically and concretely as possible, to make sure the nature of the disagreement or issue is clear. For example:
  - "Late" means more than 5 minutes.
  - "Confidential" means that the information involved must not be repeated to anyone else.
  - Any generalization must be supported by three or more examples.

The Krazy Kounselor Speaks

"When we get into an argument," the young couple told the Krazy Kounselor, "we can't seem to stop. What can we do?"

"It is very difficult to laugh and to be angry at the same time," the Krazy Kounselor said. "So to break yourselves out of the prison of anger, bring in humor."

"What are you talking about?" the couple asked.

"Tell jokes; read jokes from a joke book; watch a funny, slapstick style of movie; make faces at each other; play recorded track of laughter, applause, or funny sounds (belching, breaking wind, etc.).

"That's crazy," the young people said.

> **Laughter is medicine for the soul.**
> —Proverb

Scriptures for Meditation

"This you know, my beloved brethren. But everyone must be quick to hear, slow to speak and slow to anger; for the anger of man does not achieve the righteousness of God." —James 1:19-20

"Now the deeds of the flesh are evident, which are: immorality, impurity, sensuality, idolatry, sorcery, enmities, strife, jealousy, outbursts of anger, disputes, dissensions, factions, envying, drunkenness, carousing, and things like these, of which I forewarn you, just as I have forewarned you, that those who practice such things will not inherit the kingdom of God." —Galatians 5:19-21

My Takeaway

Think about what you have learned. What is the most important thing you will take from this chapter? What is your "action item"?

✠
✠ ✠
Prayer

LORD, please help us to remember that anger is corrosive and destructive to thinking, feeling, hearing, understanding, and deciding. Whatever the nature of our disagreement or of the hurt caused, help us to be calm, respectful, and reasonable in our discussion. May we always remember that our long-term relationship with each other is more important than any short-term problem. We thank you in Jesus' name. Amen.

✠

10
A soothing tongue is a tree of life,
But perversion in it crushes the spirit.
—Proverbs 15:4

You have no doubt noticed how many of these Biblical proverbs involve the power of talking. That's because words have impact.

Ask yourself, of all the words you speak to your spouse in a day or a week, what percentage are positive, complimentary, uplifting, supportive words and what percentage are negative, critical, contentious, contradicting words?

Next question: Would you say you are interested in energizing your marriage or are you interested in crushing its spirit?

Logic problem. See if you can understand these two formulas (trigonometry and calculus are not needed):

> *Happy Wife = Happy Husband*
> *Happy Husband = Happy Wife*

Final Exam: True or False. You can make yourself happier and more fulfilled by making your spouse miserable.

✠ ◆ ✠

Discussion Questions
1. In your experience with friends, parents, and married couples, what percentage of each communication involves building up or soothing or supporting or encouraging the other person?
2. It's been said that criticizing—finding fault—is more esteemed in our culture than praising. Do you agree? If so, why do you think this is?
3. In your own relationships, do you find it easier to criticize (or think negative thoughts) than to praise? Why or why not?

Quotation for Discussion
"Just keep in mind that you were not put on this earth for the express purpose of pointing out all your partner's mistakes." —Laura Schlessinger, *Ten Stupid Things Couples Do to Mess Up Their Relationships,* page 118

Poisonous Stems
Statements that begin with the following stems always have toxic flowers—you can feel the anger in the stem itself:

> You always . . .
> You never . . .
> I can't believe that you would . . .
> How could you ever think . . .
> Don't you ever . . .
> How dare you . . .
> You are constantly . . .
> Why can't you ever . . .

Additional Commentary
John Gottman and his team ran a 20-year study of older couples. They noted that more of the couples

who had marriages with constant conflict dropped out of the study than did couples with happy marriages. Further research revealed that, at the end of the study, of those couples in adversarial marriages, 58 percent of the husbands were dead, while of those couples in cooperative marriages, 23 percent of the husbands had died. —Gottman, *What Makes Love Last?*, page 228

Scriptures for Discussion

"But I tell you that every careless word that people speak, they shall give an accounting for it in the day of judgment. For by your words you will be justified, and by your words you will be condemned."

—Matthew 12:36-37

"Now if we put the bits into the horses' mouths so that they will obey us, we direct their entire body as well. Look at the ships also, though they are so great and are driven by strong winds, are still directed by a very small rudder wherever the inclination of the pilot desires.

"So also the tongue is a small part of the body, and yet it boasts of great things. See how great a forest is set aflame by such a small fire! And the tongue is a fire, the very world of iniquity; the tongue is set among our members as that which defiles the entire body, and sets on fire the course of our life, and is set on fire by hell.

"For every species of beasts and birds, of reptiles and creatures of the sea, is tamed and has been tamed by the human race. But no one can tame the tongue; it is a restless evil and full of deadly poison. With it we bless our Lord and Father, and with it we curse men, who have been made in the likeness of God; from the same mouth come both blessing

and cursing. My brethren, these things ought not to be this way."
—James 3:3-10

My Takeaway
Think about what you have learned. What is the most important thing you will take from this chapter? What is your "action item"?

☩
☩ ☩
Prayer

LORD, our tongues live in slippery places and always seem eager to lash out and attack someone, causing who knows how much damage. But there is a better way. Help us, dear God, to stop our mouths from spewing gossip, criticism, complaint, and resentment, and instead to remember your word that tells us, "A soothing tongue is a tree of life." When, in the resurrection, we are called to give account for "every careless word" we have spoken, may there be fewer rather than more to forgive us for. We ask this in Jesus' name. Amen.

The Voice of Experience
Asked, What was something important you learned about marriage early on, a 98-year-old widow said,
> **"Happiness doesn't just appear—
> you have to produce it."**

☩

11
Better is a dish of vegetables where love is,
Than a fattened ox and hatred with it.
—Proverbs 15:17

Marriage is only slightly about money, food, possessions, sex, and children. It's mostly about living a cooperative adventure.

The real power and value in marriage is the emotional and spiritual bond between husband and wife that makes this cooperative adventure possible, and even enjoyable. Marriage is about an emotional relationship, a spiritual communion, a psychic partnership, a team of two friends who have each other's back.

That's why this proverb tells us that vegetables served with a side order of love beats steak with a side order of hatred any day of the week.

> **Better is a little with the fear of the LORD**
> **Than great treasure and turmoil with it.**
> **—Proverbs 15:16**

✠ ♦ ✠

Discussion Questions
1. How would you define *love* in practical terms?
2. What does it mean to say that "love is a verb"?
3. Pair up with your spouse and have each person

(1) write three sentences, each beginning with the words, "Love is. . . . Next, write and three more sentences, each beginning with "Love is not. . . ." Discuss and defend your choices.

Quotation for Discussion

"The love I'm talking about experiencing that day was clear-eyed and grounded in companionship. We were Allies, Comrades, Partners, Companions. . . . This was the reality of being together as husband and wife not only in love, but in friendship.
—Les and Leslie Parrott, "Be Your Partner's Best Friend" in *The Best Advice I Ever Got on Marriage,* page 47

Scripture

"This is My commandment, that you love one another, just as I have loved you."

—John 15:12 (NASB)

Defining Love

Discuss the following characteristics of love, below.
1. Which are the top three most important?
2. Which are the three least important?
3. Which are the most ignored?
4. Which do you focus on in your relationships?
5. Which are the easiest to practice?
6. Which involve the greatest challenge to practice?

Acceptance. Entire, open-hearted welcoming. Not "putting up with" some things, or viewing some trait of personality with a secret disgust. But always mentally embracing the other—from phobias to pimples.

Compassion. Never feeling contempt or scorn for any sincere human being striving for virtue and truth, or for one who would strive if he could, or knew how. Sympathizing with pains and distresses, though you cannot feel or even understand them, and being disturbed until you can alleviate them.

Selflessness. Turning aside from self-interest and being willing to give without hope or desire of return. Sacrificing because you know someone else needs it. A humble, generous desire to offer up yourself and to do good things because good things ought to be done, not because you expect gratitude or a reward.

Understanding. A gentle and unsuperior tolerance of a soul different from yours, yet with cares and concerns, hopes and fears, desires and expectations equally powerful with yours, and felt with equal or greater pain or joy.

Caring. An almost instinctive concern for the welfare and happiness of a being, made in the image of God, especially placed in your life or under your protection, to be valued and cherished more than your eyes, more than your breath, more than your favorite folly.

Encouragement. A willing and active support. Adding your light to extend the vision, and your hand to assure the steps. Praising little victories, knowing that all great conquests come from them. Changing the orientation of the entire world by saying, simply, "You're right, and I'm with you."

Forgiveness. Letting go of wrongs, forgetting hurts, holding no grudges. The freshness of forgiveness erasing past offenses. Welcoming the forgiven into open, unconditionally loving arms, and making all things new.

Kindness. A warm focus on the needs of another, helping with a friendly gentleness, with happy generosity, and with unassuming grace.

> **Secret Key #4 to a Happy Marriage**
> Love is something you do
> Even more than something you feel.

Additional Commentary

The food imagery in this Proverb is relevant to the nature of the marriage relationship. Just as a meal lasts only a few hours before you need to eat again, thus making your life a collection of many meals, so marriage is a collection of many interactions. For each interaction, you can choose anew what it will be like. Just because the last interaction was unpleasant (because someone didn't eat some humble pie?), doesn't doom the spouses (or siblings!) to the same thing next time. Choose something different to eat and your digestion might improve.

My Takeaway

Think about what you have learned. What is the most important thing you will take from this chapter? What is your "action item"?

✠
✠ ✠

Prayer

Dear LORD, you model love for us everywhere. You show us sacrificial love in the willingness of Jesus to die in our place; you show us practical love through the teaching of the Holy Spirit, and his reminders to live the way we know we should. And you show us fatherly love yourself through the blessings, grace, and mercy that you continue to heap upon us. LORD, make us imitators of all that love, as we relate to our spouses and to others. We thank you in the name of Jesus. Amen.

✠

12
Pride goes before destruction,
And a haughty spirit before stumbling.
—Proverbs 16:18

What does this proverb have to do with marriage, you may ask? Well, a major problem with some couples is that they can't get out from under their own egos so that they can simply enjoy their spouse and their marriage.

Want to have a happy marriage? Humble yourself, stop trying to control your spouse or to make your spouse into someone exactly like you. Instead, serve your spouse's needs.

> **See Appendix 3: The Keys to Happiness.**

Just as life in general is not about you, so marriage is not about you, either. Marriage is not a relationship you enter merely for what you can get out of it. Relationships are built through mutual sacrifice and service, with both partners kicking pride off the throne.

To paraphrase President Kennedy, "Ask not what your marriage can do for you; ask what you can do for your marriage."

✠ ♦ ✠

Discussion Questions
1. It is often said that pride—or arrogance or egotism—is really a mask that insecure people wear, to protect their self-doubts or to boost their egos. Based on your experience, what is your assessment of this claim?
2. In what sense is a "haughty spirit" a prelude to stumbling?
3. What is the secret to breaking the cycle of insecurity? (See the Additional Commentary, below, and "Overcoming the Vicious Cycle of Insecurity," in Appendix 8.)

Quotation for Discussion
". . . It is not unusual for people who have suffered to take it out on their spouses—a kind of 'I suffered at the hands of another so now you owe me!' mentality. . . . Carrying over old problems into marriage and family is a selfishness borne of unresolved anger and hurts; nonetheless, it is a self-centeredness: me, my hurts . . . you won't get me! . . . Happiness and love are not gotten by force of will, nor are they automatically granted simply because you show up. The greatest amount of getting is through giving . . . When it's me or you, it's a fight. When it's you and me in the sight of God, it's a festival."
—Laura Schlessinger, *Ten Stupid Things Couples Do to Mess Up Their Relationships,* pages 64, 67, 70, 71

Additional Commentary and Questions
Many problems in relationships can be traced back ultimately to insecurities developed in childhood. Note the continuum in the table below.
1. What are some ways to attack these insecurities?
2. How can you avoid creating a monster prideful ego?

Insecurity and Pride

Insecurity	**I'm afraid I don't measure up.** Dad always said I'd never amount to anything and Mom was an obsessive tyrant. And my friends at school called me a loser.
↓ **Leads to** **Need to Boost Ego**	**I matter** (Oh, and then there's you). **I'm special** (Me first you maybe later). I'm better than others (including you). I'm confident (but you're controlling). This is all about me (I'll do everything for me and you can, too).
↓ **Leads to** **Power Struggle**	**I'm in charge** (Why ask you?). One upping (I can do anything better than you). Anger (How dare you offend me and my righteous knowledge of the truth?). You can't tell me what to do (I'm not part of the team).
↓ **Leads to** **Controlling Behavior**	**I am always right** (You're stupid). **You're second class** (We're not equals and you need to know your place). Nitpicking (You missed a spot). Criticism (You're broken and you're not good enough).
↓ **Leads to** **Pride**	**Rework** Doing tasks over and over again (You're incompetent).

Additional Scripture
"Why do you look at the speck that is in your brother's eye, but do not notice the log that is in your own eye? Or how can you say to your brother, 'Let me take the speck out of your eye,' and behold, the log is in your own eye? You hypocrite, first take the log out of your own eye, and then you will see clearly to take the speck out of your brother's eye."
—Matthew 7:3-5

Think and Respond
What message does one person send to the other by the actions described below? How is the recipient likely to respond?
1. One mows the lawn. The other looks at it, scowls, and mows the lawn again, the "right way."
2. One loads the dishwasher. The other looks at it, says it's all wrong, and reloads it the "right way."
3. One cleans the counter. The other comes in, looks, and says, "I thought you said you cleaned the counter. The first says, "I did." The other says, "You must be joking," and cleans the counter again, the "right way."

Quotations for Thought
Worried about what others think? For those whose self-esteem is tied up in the opinion of others, Thomas a Kempis, author of the classic *Imitation of Christ*, wrote (paraphrased here), "Do not allow your sense of self-worth or inner peace to be controlled by the opinions of other people. Whatever they say or think of you, good or bad, their opinion does not make you another person. Instead, you are who you are."

Too proud to humble yourself? Think about it: Do you want to go through life filled with pride and arrogance, or filled with joy and friendship?

Just how great do you think you are? The very wise 18th Century writer Samuel Johnson once commented to his friend James Boswell, "There is nothing, Sir, too little for so little a creature as man."

Grow up and think about someone other than yourself.

Scripture
"What do you have that God hasn't given you? And if everything you have is from God, why boast as though it were not a gift?" —1 Corinthians 4:7 (NLT)

My Takeaway
Think about what you have learned. What is the most important thing you will take from this chapter? What is your "action item"?

✠
✠ ✠
PRAYER
Dear LORD, we ask that you will help us to realize that pride is the sin of fools. Help us to humble ourselves by reminding us that every good attribute we have—intelligence, beauty, strength, wealth, power, achievements—all are gifts from you. Remind us that, on this planet of billions of people, there are thousands of others who out class us in whatever thing we are tempted to use to puff ourselves up. Guide us as we employ—with gratitude rather than egotism—the undeserved gifts you have given us. In Jesus' name. Amen.

✠

13
Bright eyes gladden the heart.
—Proverbs 15:30a

This proverb is a reminder that when you and your spouse meet again after being separated by the workday or any other reason, you should make an effort to put on your happy face and cheerful tone, reflecting the joy of reunion, and showing that you are glad to meet again.

In every reunion, the first 30 seconds are crucial. Your husband or wife will lock in what appears to be your mood and will interpret your subsequent comments and actions by that initial appearance.

Greeting your spouse with bright eyes sets the right tone. And adding a meaningful hug or kiss couldn't hurt, either.

The opposite, of course, greeting your spouse with a grumpy, out-of-sorts tone of voice and a scowl, will not gladden the heart. In fact, such a demeanor warns, "I'm in a bad mood."

And men, being the simple creatures they are, believe that, when their wives adopt this grumpy behavior, the real message is, "I'm in a bad mood, and it's your fault."

✠ ◆ ✠

Discussion Questions
1. The commentary says spouses should "make an effort to put on a happy face and a cheerful tone" when they reunite after being apart. But what if the day was a disaster?
2. If you greet your spouse (child, friend) with an unhappy, frustrated, frowning demeanor, what is that person likely to think?

Joke for Discussion

Wife: "I don't think you love me anymore."
Husband: "Why do you say that?"
Wife: "You never tell me you love me."
Husband: "I told you at our wedding that I love you."
Wife: "That was forty years ago."
Husband: "Well, I haven't changed my mind, but if I do, I'll let you know."

[Adapted from *14 Secretes to a Better Marriage* by Dave Earley, page 114]

Scripture
"So when it was evening on that day, the first day of the week, and when the doors were shut where the disciples were, for fear of the Jews, Jesus came and stood in their midst and said to them, 'Peace be with you.'" —John 20:19

Additional Commentary
We should all strive to have bright eyes, not just for our spouse and friends, but for everyone, as an emblem of the joy we have in Christ. It's not a very good model or witness to be glum or angry or negative people of the faith. As Samuel Johnson said in *Rambler* No. 44, "Remember that the greatest honor you can pay to the author of your being is by such a cheerful behavior as discovers a mind satisfied with his dispensations."

The Krazy Kounselor Speaks

The people complained to the Krazy Kounselor, "Our jobs tire us out and create so much stress that when we get home, we don't have the energy to put on a cheerful mood. We can't help but be somber, or downright grumpy. What can we do?"

The Krazy Kounselor replied, "It is a common problem for highly industrious workers to tighten their bolts so hard that the machinery begins to wear on itself and those nearby. The parts cannot flex enough to rest. They are too serious."

"What?" the people said. "We're not asking about machinery."

"Does he mean 'belts'?" someone asked.

"There is no joy in grief or anger," said the Krazy Kounselor. "An unhappy couple should give each other a massage, a back rub, and love—tell some jokes and laugh each other back to sanity."

"That's crazy," the people said.

My Takeaway

Think about what you have learned. What is the most important thing you will take from this chapter? What is your "action item"?

✠

✠ ✠

Prayer

LORD, please help us to feel and to reflect in our behavior the joy we have in you. Keep us from projecting an attitude of disgruntlement and dissatisfaction with the events of our lives and the people we interact with. May we instead be a source of encouragement and edification, showing everyone the love of Christ through our behavior. In Jesus' name we thank you. Amen.

✠

14
Pleasant words are a honeycomb,
Sweet to the soul and healing to the bones.
—Proverbs 16:24

Successful marriage is the result of an emotional partnership. Kind words, encouragement, and support are the glue that holds the marriage together. Think of marriage as a friendship taken to the next level.

Note how the right words can build up your spouse:

> Supporting words = Stronger relationship
> Kind words = Contentment
> Complimentary words = Inspiration
> Encouraging words = Confidence
> Approving words = Harmony
> Forgiving words = Healing
> Reassuring words = Security

In a culture that obsesses with failure and criticism, where gentle and loving words are rare, pleasant words from one's spouse do more to make a marriage happy than just about any other thing.

Oh, and don't forget to clothe those words in a warm tone of voice.

✠ ◆ ✠

Discussion Questions
1. Why is such importance placed on using "pleasant words" such as compliments and encouragements with one's spouse or friend?
2. How would you respond to someone who said that deliberately using positive expressions was "patronizing, phony, and serving canned mush"?
3. Why, do you think, that "I need you" is listed among the Magic Words in Appendix 2?

Activity
What other pleasant words or phrases can you think of that friends and spouses could use with each other? (Think of categories, if that will help: praise, encouragement, gratitude, affection.)

Words that Support and Encourage
Appendix 2 lists many phrases, called "The Magic Words," that will help you build a very strong, confident, happy relationship. Saying these phrases to your spouse regularly (some should be said daily) will remind him or her of your support, trust, and love.

> **Secret Key #5 to a Happy Marriage**
> Use the Magic Words Frequently

Quotation for Discussion
"Marriages that are healthy, where you are confident that you can be secure and succeed, are characterized by mutual affection. You go out of your way to compliment one another. You find ways to encourage each other:

"You can cultivate affection in your marriage by kindly touching one another, by focusing on

your spouse's unique ability, and by showering your relationship with kind words."
—Bill and Pam Farrel, *The Marriage Code,* page 52

Scripture
"Therefore encourage one another and build up one another, just as you also are doing."
—1 Thessalonians 5:11

My Takeaway
Think about what you have learned. What is the most important thing you will take from this chapter? What is your "action item"?

✠
✠ ✠
PRAYER
LORD, you know that for many of us, among our favorite Scriptures are those that express your love and affection, such as, "I have called you friends," and, "Abide in my love." Help us to transfer the joy and love we feel from reading these words into expressions of love and joy for our spouse. And may we never forget that we represent Christ to each other. In Jesus' name we thank you. Amen.

The Voice of Experience
Asked, How have you remained happily married for so many years? a 92-year-old husband and his 89-year-old wife said,
"Build each other up through kindness."

✞

15
Better is a dry morsel and quietness with it
Than a house full of feasting with strife.
—Proverbs 17:1

The home should be a sanctuary where husband and wife can join together in peace and security, safe from the tensions and stresses of the day.

Home should be a place of mutual support, an alliance, not a combat zone.

All of us need a place and a friend where together we can "let our hair down," relax, decompress, and regain our sanity and our sense of self—including our sense of self-worth.

When the house is not a place to exhale and relax the tense muscles—when the opposite of a sanctuary is present—the feelings of tension and strife grow larger, and the entire person grows weaker, as does the relationship itself.

Save that attitude of "crush the competition" for the boardroom or tennis court. Don't bring it home with you.

✠ ◆ ✠

Discussion Questions
1. Why does arguing while eating create an especially problematic situation?
2. Why is quietness so important to a relationship?

3. Think of several expressions that refer to taking time to relax in quietness and peace, and discuss their implications. Examples: *chill out, vegetate, unplug and drift, recharge the batteries.*

Scripture
Let your adornment be "the hidden person of the heart, with the imperishable quality of a gentle and quiet spirit, which is precious in the sight of God."
—1 Peter 3:4

Word Study
Discuss how the additional possible meanings of the Hebrew words add richness and depth to the proverb.

Quietness = Hebrew *shalvah*. Definition: quietness, ease, peace, security, prosperity, time of tranquility (Strong's 7962)

Strife = Hebrew *riyb*. Definition: strife, complaint, contend, contention, dispute, quarrel, adversary, contest, chiding, lawsuit (Strong's 7379)

The Ten Rules of Good Discussion Etiquette
Whether you are dreaming about a fabulous vacation or trying to solve a serious interpersonal problem, observing these rules for a successful and lower stress discussion will help keep things under control and improve the interaction.

1. **Use a neutral tone of voice.** If you speak with a negative or critical tone of voice, you imply that the other person is wrong or even stupid and not worth being taken seriously. Nothing will prolong an argument, prevent progress. or inhibit basic communication as fast as that sneering, disbelieving, mocking tone of voice.
2. **Avoid mockery, ridicule, and sarcasm.** Such built-in contempt for the other person will prevent solving the problem.

3. **Listen to the other person.** Don't just wait for the other person to pause so that you can offer your next point or a rebuttal of the person's last point. Listen to gain understanding of the other's point of view and reasons.
4. **Ask questions.** Ask honest questions to get details or clarification — and not to create "gotcha" situations. Use a sincere tone. Incorporate the answers into your understanding of the other person's viewpoint.
5. **Restate and summarize the other person's position fairly.** Do not create straw man, distorted, or extreme versions of the person's ideas. Avoid that common, counterproductive tactic of exaggerating and even falsifying the other person's idea, prefixed by, "So what you're saying is. . . ." Sentences that begin this way almost never reflect an accurate or honest paraphrase and are seen through as merely attacks. They tell the other person that you are not really interested in their ideas.[2]
6. **Don't interrupt the speaker.** Interrupting another person in the middle of a discussion conveys the message that you believe that what they have to say is unimportant. Interrupting on a constant basis conveys contempt.
7. **Don't talk over the other person.** Continuing to talk while another person is talking indicates that no one is listening and that therefore the conversation is a futile exercise in venting, not intended to gain understanding or agreement.
8. **Don't raise your voice.** Raising your voice, not necessarily even to the point of shouting, conveys to the other person that you have run out

---

[2] See Appendix 9 for more information about logical fallacies to avoid when arguing.

of good arguments or evidence, that you have no respect for the other person, and even that you might become violent soon. If you can't remain calm and polite, you should stop the discussion until you cool down.

9. **Don't be a motormouth.** Don't hog the conversation. If you really want progress in the discussion, pause after every sentence or two to allow the listener to answer, ask, state, agree, clarify, object, or inject whatever response he or she wants. Listeners to long, non-stop diatribes feel as if they are not getting a reasoned presentation, but a verbal beating—because that's just what they are getting.

10. **Don't change the subject.** If you change the subject in the middle of a discussion, your listener will conclude that you realize that you are losing the argument and so you are arbitrarily shifting to another topic that you hope you can "win," implying that you consider the discussion to be a game or competition whose goal is for one person to win, rather than seeing it as a joint effort where the two of you can solve a problem, come to an agreement, develop a plan of action, or clarify each other's position.

Group Activity
1. Discuss the Ten Rules of Good Discussion Etiquette and explain how following each rule improves the quality of the conversation.
2. Explain how violating each rule hurts the effectiveness of a discussion.
3. Have the group rank order the Ten Rules from most important to least important. Watch over the discussion carefully to be sure that none of the Rules are violated during the process.

4. Choose one rule and have each member of the group supply a new example that violates the rule. Then as a group rank the examples from most serious violation of the Rule to least serious. Watch over the discussion carefully to be sure that none of the rules are violated during the process of ranking.
5. The Eleventh Rule. Is there a missing rule that would make conversations more successful and productive? Describe that rule and discuss its usefulness. Include examples.

Vignette
Explain the meaning of this vignette.

> As the bride and groom ran down the church steps, dodging the rice thrown by their well-wishers, the voice of an old man could just barely be heard over the cheering:
>
> "May you have many discussions, few debates, and no arguments."

My Takeaway
Think about what you have learned. What is the most important thing you will take from this chapter? What is your "action item"?

✠
✠ ✠
PRAYER
LORD, thank you for creating the marriage relationship, that allows us to form an alliance with each other and live in a place where rest and recovery can take place after each day's challenges. May we always be grateful to you and to each other for our fortress against the storm. In Jesus' name. Amen.

16
The contentions of a wife
Are a constant dripping.
—Proverbs 19:13b

If the book of Proverbs had been written by a woman, this proverb would probably say something like, "The stubbornness of a man is like an ox stuck in the mud." The difference tells us about men and women.

A man with a contentious wife feels rejected and incompetent because she seems to him to imply that he is always wrong. A woman with a stubborn husband feels devalued because he seems to her to refuse to validate her feelings and needs.

You can see that each one's behavior reinforces the other's behavior.

Remedy:

Wives. Stop trying to fix, change, or improve your husbands, especially by nagging. Your mission in life is not to search out your husband's every fault and comment on it. (Look up *forbearance* in the dictionary.)

Husbands. Listen to your wives and take them seriously. They are not talking just to heat up the room. Think about what they say and allow yourselves to be influenced by them.

Discussion Questions
1. Someone has said that in many marriages, the reason for contentiousness is that, while the couple love each other, they are not (yet) friends. What is your response to this idea?
2. Reflect on the Friend poster below and discuss what makes friendship. How is friendship different from love?

Quotation for Discussion
The following quotation offers a perspective on a common failing among married people: the tendency to whine, criticize, and express dissatisfaction with their spouse. Why is this behavior so widespread? How is it harmful to the relationship?

"We will not put each other down. When I've failed . . . I couldn't ask for a greater friend . . . to lean on than Betty. But the happiness in our marriage hasn't sprung from always meeting each other's expectations. On the contrary, we both have failed many times to live up to the other's expectations. But even in those disappointments, rather than adding to the load of the shortcoming or failure, we immediately begin to try to unload the boat, lighten each other's load, and lift each other up."

—James and Betty Robison, *Living in Love*, pages 213-214

You be the Counselor
Counsel this couple:
> Dale: "It turned out to be a bit cloudy today."
>
> Loren: "No it isn't. There's way more blue sky than clouds."
>
> Dale: "Look how crowded the sidewalks are. People are really jammed."
>
> Loren: "That's not crowded. That's nothing compared to the Walking Street last Christmas."
>
> Dale: "Maybe I should stop and get gas, in case we decide to drive farther than Willets."
>
> Loren: "There's no need to stop. You've got a quarter of a tank. That's plenty."
>
> Dale: "Shall we have breakfast at the Golden Waffle? I love their breakfasts."
>
> Loren: "I hate that place. Go to the Supreme Pancake House."
>
> Dale: "Okay. I'll just turn here."
>
> Loren: "Where do you think you're going? The way to the restaurant is to go down 4th Street."
>
> Dale: "The Diagonal goes through to Main, so it's almost a short cut."
>
> Loren: "Well, that's stupid. But do what you want. There's no contradicting you. And you always have to get your way."

Scripture

"My dear friends, as a follower of our Lord Jesus Christ, I beg you to get along with each other. Don't take sides. Always try to agree in what you think."
—1 Corinthians 1:10 (CEV)

My Takeaway

Think about what you have learned. What is the most important thing you will take from this chapter? What is your "action item"?

✠
✠ ✠

Prayer

LORD, please help us as husband and wife—as true friends—to support and encourage each other, not tear each other down. Help us to edify each other, not to shame each other. May we always remember that even though life is filled with many battles and struggles, with your help and our commitment to each other to fight them side by side, we can be victorious. Remind us when necessary that we are fighting together, not against each other. We pray this and thank you in Jesus' name. Amen.

✠

17
He who finds a wife finds a good thing,
And obtains favor from the LORD
—Proverbs 18:22

In a loving, Biblical marriage, a wife truly is a blessing from the Lord, a blessing that continues to grow and deepen and enrich as time goes on.

Like any other "good thing," however, this blessing requires care and maintenance. If the blessing were a car, men would understand this, paying close attention to its needs, buying it toys, and bragging about it. They know that the better the maintenance, the more reliable the car. Neglect paying attention to service, and your car just might let you down.

So, husbands, keep your wife a "good thing," by providing the care she needs. Listen when she needs to talk, be considerate of her needs, reassure her regularly that you love her and that you care about her happiness.

Give her some flowers on an ordinary day for no special reason at all—other than that you love her.

✠ ◆ ✠

Discussion Questions
1. What are some things a husband can do to provide "better maintenance" for his wife?

2. Why do some men have a tendency to neglect their wives, or their relationship with their wives? Is it because men and women do not understand their differences?
3. The analogy between maintaining a woman and maintaining a car might seem odd to some people. Can you think of a better one?
4. If husbands and wives took seriously the proverb's statement that a wife represents "favor from the Lord," how would each of their attitudes and behaviors toward each other be affected?
5. Referring to the table below, discuss the differences between men and women. What problems occur when men and women are said to be the same?

Differences Between Men and Women

Characteristic	Men	Women	Source of Conflict
Life Focus	Goals	Relationships	Accomplishment vs Friendship
Memory Style	Gist or Sum	Details	The Point vs The Details
Primary Motive	Feeling needed, respected, honored	Feeling cherished, loved, safe, secure	Assuming their own motive is the same as their spouse's
Types of Love Needed	Trust, Acceptance, Appreciation, Admiration, Approval, Encouragement	Caring, Understanding, Valuing, Validation, Reassurance, Empathy	Thinking that spouse's needs are the same as one's own needs

Quotation for Discussion
"Remind yourself that being helpful to each other will do far more for the strength and passion of your marriage than a two-week Bahamas getaway."
—John Gottman, *Seven Principles*, pages 82-83

Fundamental Needs of Wives Discussion
Read the section on Wives in Appendix 6, and then discuss (1) how well the section defines wives' needs, (2) whether the men in the group were aware of these needs, and (3) what changes in behavior the men in the discussion now plan to make.

My Takeaway
Think about what you have learned. What is the most important thing you will take from this chapter? What is your "action item"?

✠
✠ ✠
Prayer
LORD, we thank you for making your creatures male and female, with our similarities that we might love and support each other, and with our differences that we might complement each other through our varied perspectives on life and its events. Help us always to remember that we are allies and not enemies, that we are on the same team, though we play different positions, and that our goal in life is to help each other to serve you and to build up our brothers and sisters in the faith. In Jesus' name we thank you. Amen.

✠

18
What is desirable in a man is his kindness.
—Proverbs 19:22a

If I had to guess, I'd say this is the proverb that wives will pick out as their favorite among the others quoted in this book.

Husbands, what's the deal here? Can you be a little more effortful and deliberate in showing kindness—and appreciation—to your wives? A little softer, not so gruff, not so demanding? And how about consulting her more often when you face those larger decisions? Remember, she's your partner.

Being head of the household doesn't give you license to be controlling, bossy, or commandeering, much less mean and cruel.

So, how about lightening up? How about being thoughtful and generous (bought her any earrings lately?), or as the proverb says, being kind?

And, for heaven's sake, can you pick up your socks and underwear and put the toilet seat down?

✠ ◆ ✠

Discussion Questions
1. What is the relationship between kindness and love? (Consider the proverb: "Kindness is the right arm of love.")

2. Comment on the proverb, "The opposite of kindness is not cruelty; it is thoughtlessness."
3. Recall the first Proverb quoted in this book, Proverbs 3:3-4. "Do not let kindness and truth leave you. . . ." Comment.

Scripture Bouquet for Discussion

"Therefore, return to your God, Observe kindness and justice, And wait for your God continually." —Hosea 12:6

"He has told you, O man, what is good; And what does the LORD require of you But to do justice, to love kindness, And to walk humbly with your God?" —Micah 6:8

"Thus has the LORD of hosts said, 'Dispense true justice and practice kindness and compassion each to his brother; and do not oppress the widow or the orphan, the stranger or the poor; and do not devise evil in your hearts against one another.'"
—Zechariah 7:9-10

"But the fruit of the Spirit is love, joy, peace, patience, kindness, goodness, faithfulness, gentleness, self-control; against such things there is no law." —Galatians 5:22-23

"So, as those who have been chosen of God, holy and beloved, put on a heart of compassion, kindness, humility, gentleness and patience; bearing with one another, and forgiving each other, whoever has a complaint against anyone; just as the Lord forgave you, so also should you."
—Colossians 3:13-14

Quotation for Discussion

"I often ask husbands, 'Does your wife love you?' They reply, 'Yes, of course.' But then I ask, 'Does she like you?' And the answer usually comes back, 'Nope.'"

"In many cases, the wife's dislike is interpreted by the husband as disrespect and even contempt…. She doesn't approve, and she's letting him know it. So the husband decides he will motivate his wife to become more respectful by acting in unloving ways."
—Emerson Eggerichs, *Love and Respect*, pages 17-18

Additional Commentary

By now you have noticed how important kindness is to the successful and happy operation of a marriage. By mentioning men specifically, this proverb reminds us that men are often the less kind member of the marital partnership. As with so many things in life, intentionality makes the difference between the success and the failure of any goal.

Below is the Man Mirror, a list of behavioral cues to help men be intentional about exhibiting kindness toward their wives.

THE MAN MIRROR

Kind
Warm
Edifying
Pleasant
Cheerful
Thoughtful
Cordial
Genial
Benevolent
Considerate
Mindful
Helpful
Understanding
Sympathetic
Empathetic

1. Explain how an ordinary man can embody the Man Mirror characteristics while still modeling the virtues of courage, wisdom, strength, assertiveness, and tenacity.
2. Of the kindness concepts in the "Man Mirror" poster, which one seems especially important to you? Why?
3. Define five, ten, or all of the words in the Man Mirror poster. Give three brief examples of each, demonstrating how they might be put into practice.

> **Do a Random Act of Kindness**
> Praise your spouse in the presence of others.

My Takeaway
Think about what you have learned. What is the most important thing you will take from this chapter? What is your "action item"?

✠
✠ ✠
Prayer

Dear LORD, when we get home from work or an appointment, eager to join together with our spouse in renewed comfort and friendship, help us to lay aside the aggressions and hardnesses necessitated by the day, and put on the robe of kindness. Enable us to provide the balm of softness, sympathy, and approval that our spouse has come to need. And may we always reflect the love our Savior Jesus gives us, pouring out gentle goodness and love from a ready supply. In his name we pray. Amen.

✠

19
It is better to live in a desert land,
Than with a contentious and vexing woman.
—Proverbs 21:19

In order to understand why the book of Proverbs contains a number of similar sayings about contentious and vexing wives, several factors need to be taken into consideration.

First, men are much more sensitive, with their fragile eggshell egos, than their wives probably believe is possible for such supposedly rugged creatures. But the truth is, criticism and conflict from one's hoped-for ally and supporter can hurt a man deeply.

Second, wives who vex their husbands by constantly arguing with them might not intend to send the message of rejection and disrespect that their husbands are receiving. If you're in doubt about how your husband perceives you, try this. At some opportune moment in a casual conversation, say, "I agree completely." Your husband's reaction will tell you everything you need to know.

See Appendix 2: The Magic Words

If you can't find an opportune moment to say those words, that will also tell you something.

(If you say them and like the reaction, use them regularly, together with the other Magic Words. See Appendix 2.)

Men have a profound need to feel competent and, just like women, a need to feel validated. Contentiousness prevents these feelings from growing and blossoming in a man's heart.

The takeaway from the above is that poor communication—poor understanding of the intended message—is perhaps the largest cause of marital disharmony, argument, hurt, confusion, and unhappiness.

Wives can be less contentious and less vexing by

- Looking for points of agreement rather than disagreement.
- Reassuring their husbands that the comments are in the context of love and respect.
- Not commenting on every tiny issue

Husbands can help their wives to avoid contentiousness and vexing by

- Responding to their wives' legitimate complaints.
- Attending to "honey, do" requests in a timely way.

✠ ◆ ✠

Discussion Questions

1. What do you think is the reason behind conten-

tiousness in any relationship?
2. How can contentiousness be remedied — or at least addressed and reduced?

Talking and Listening

It is sometimes said that many people simply do not know how to hold a satisfying and productive conversation. (When young people were asked, "What is the purpose of a discussion?" most of them said, "To prove the other person wrong.")

Read and discuss these descriptions of productive and unproductive conversational types.

Monologue

Description. Non-stop talker lecturing, venting, scolding, making a speech, orating. Logorrhea, continuous verbal torrent, a fire hose of words in the ear. Talker does not seem to believe that pauses are useful.

Typical Content. The listener is limited to token signs of listening: uh huh, yeah, oh, okay, got it, mm hmm

Impact and Effects. The listener is subjected to the orator's control and harangue, causing hearing fatigue because of verbal overload. If the speaker is arguing a point, the listener remains unconvinced because of cognitive overload or failure to have objections or questions addressed.

Talking Past Each Other

Description. Two very verbal talkers, interrupting each other, talking over each other.

Typical Content. Dual verbal streams, nearly independent.

Impact and Effects. Each talker is absorbed in his or her own world, addressing a somewhat different issue or using different definitions of the same words. Neither pays much attention to the other. Raised voices not uncommon, since the goal is to be heard, not to hear.

Talking At Each Other

Description. Alternating pontifications. Pretended attention, with interruptions. Verbal combat.

Typical Content. At a pause or interruption, the listener counters, with, "But" and then presents his or her own case, disregarding the other's. Reciprocal verbal volleys.

Impact and Effects. Silent person is not listening, just waiting for the talker to pause so the silent person can talk, usually for rebuttal. Red herrings (change of topic) common. No clarity, no closure, no agreement. The goal is to make points by contradicting and proving the other person wrong. "Talking for victory."

Talking To Each Other

Description. Exchange of ideas. Actually listening and thinking about the other's statements. Open to change.

Typical Content. Questions and clarifications about meanings, values, ideas.

Impact and Effects. Each makes an effort to understand the meaning of the other's statements and vocabulary. The other's arguments are considered fairly. Communication of each one's ideas to the other occurs.

Talking With Each Other

Description. Building shared meaning, finding commonality, solving problems.

Typical Content. Each speaker paraphrases and summarizes the other's points to confirm meaning. Speakers share enthusiasm by adding ideas to each side.

Impact and Effects. Each speaker builds on the ideas or statements of the other, increasing mutual understanding. Disagreements settled by fair granting of each one's facts or points. Consensus or resolution (even agreeing to disagree) occurs.

Paraphrase of a Quotation for Discussion
James Boswell, Samuel Johnson's biographer, noted that Dr. Johnson admitted that he often "talked for victory," (that is, simply to win) rather than express what he actually believed. He would take the opposite side in a discussion and argue forcefully for it in order to humiliate his opponents.
 —James Boswell, *Life of Johnson*, April 30, 1773

Questions for Thought
1. When you have a disagreement with your spouse or friend, is it better for you to be happy or for you to be right all the time?
2. What purpose does the "habit of objection" serve? That is, what is the goal of objecting to whatever your spouse or friend says?
3. Should you always play devil's advocate when your spouse or friend makes a statement of opinion?
4. When, in a social situation among friends and strangers, your spouse makes a factual error while narrating events, do you correct your spouse in the name of truth and accuracy or allow the error to pass in order to prevent embarrassing your spouse? Explain your choice.
5. The next time you are about to disagree with or contradict your spouse, stop for a moment and ask yourself why. If you have more than one reason (that is, if you have different reasons for different circumstances), explain the various ones.

Scripture
"But now put these things out of your life: anger, losing your temper, doing or saying things to hurt others, and saying shameful things."
 —Colossians 3:8 (ERV)

My Takeaway
Think about what you have learned. What is the most important thing you will take from this chapter? What is your "action item"?

☦

☦ ☦

Prayer

Dear LORD, you have blessed us with many wonderful gifts that our experience and knowledge teach us how to enjoy. We think about the blessings of truth, love, trust, hope, and faith, and are deeply grateful to you for them because they are the stone and cement of our relationships. And we also think about our relationships themselves, as individual collections experience, for they make us feel alive in unique ways.

But there is another blessing you have made available to us, a blessing that we often forget, but which illuminates all the other blessings, and that is the blessing of understanding. As we read in Scripture, "How blessed is the man who finds wisdom and the man who gains understanding" (Proverbs 3:13).

LORD, may we always seek to understand each other, fairly and without bias. May our communications always be open and honestly seeking the truth from others, so that through accurate understanding, we may build the true and lasting foundations of relationship. In the name of Jesus, our Savior, we ask. Amen.

☦

20
A man's pride will bring him low,
But a humble spirit will obtain honor.
—Proverbs 29:23

Someday I'm going to write an entire book about pride and its horrible consequences. It will be a long, ugly book because pride is the source of a phenomenal amount of pain and heartache—needless pain and heartache. This is sadly true in some marriages, too.

Remember Jesus' teaching: "Whoever wishes to become great among you shall be your servant" (Matthew 20:26b). And Paul applies this to everyday relationships, including marriage partners: "Be willing to serve each other out of respect for Christ" (Ephesians 5:21, ERV).

So, the next time you are irritated at your spouse for a horrible crime such as chipping a dish or neglecting to put the soda back in the refrigerator, get down off your high horse and think about how blessed you are that someone would actually marry you, of all people, and go give your spouse a loving hug of gratitude.

✠ ♦ ✠

Discussion Questions
1. Why, do you think, some people are proud or act arrogantly around others?

2. Does modeling humility have any effect on the proud people who observe it?
3. Why is it important to be humble around your spouse or close friends?
4. How is it that "a humble spirit will obtain honor"?

Activity: The Seven Deadly Sins

Discuss each of the following traditional members of the Seven Deadly Sins.
1. How does each one cause problems in a marriage or other relationship?
2. How effective are the listed remedies?
3. Describe more effective remedies for each of the sins.

Sin	Remedy
Pride	Humble yourself
Anger	Never go to bed angry
Avarice	Don't be selfish and greedy
Gluttony	Stop eating while still hungry
Lust	Drink from your own cistern
Envy	Envy is a green-eyed monster
Sloth	The early bird gets the worm

Activity: Biblical Pride

In the following Scriptures (NASB version), circle all of the words and phrases relating to pride. From these sentences, what does Scripture say about the source and consequences of pride?

1. "Be of the same mind toward one another; do not be haughty in mind, but associate with the lowly. Do not be wise in your own estimation."
—Romans 12:16

2. "For through the grace given to me I say to everyone among you not to think more highly of himself than he ought to think; but to think so as to have sound judgment, as God has allotted to each a measure of faith." —Romans 12:3
3. "Haughty eyes and a proud heart, the lamp of the wicked, is sin." —Proverbs 21:4
4. "The fear of the Lord is to hate evil; pride and arrogance and the evil way and the perverted mouth, I hate." —Proverbs 8:13
5. "When pride comes, then comes dishonor, but with the humble is wisdom." —Proverbs 11:12
6. "For from within, out of the heart of men, proceed the evil thoughts, fornications, thefts, murders, adulteries, deeds of coveting and wickedness, as well as deceit, sensuality, envy, slander, pride and foolishness." —Mark 7:21-22
7. "Rise up, O judge of the earth; render recompense to the proud." —Psalm 94:2
8. "You younger men, likewise, be subject to your elders; and all of you, clothe yourselves with humility toward one another, for God is opposed to the proud, but gives grace to the humble." —1 Peter 5:5
9. "But as it is, you boast in your arrogance; all such boasting is evil." —James 4:16

Additional Commentary

Read the story below, and then discuss the questions that follow.

Why Mr. Miniver Hanged Himself[3]

Mr. and Mrs. Miniver lived in a quaint old house on Allegory Road. Their house was well kept and their

---

[3] Reprinted from Robert Harris, *Seventy Stories and a Poem*, VirtualSalt Publishing, © 2013. Used by permission.

yard was beautiful, but Mrs. Miniver mostly frowned and Mr. Miniver mostly sighed.

One day when Mrs. Miniver came home from the store, Mr. Miniver put down his screwdriver and looked out the attic window. "Did we get something good for dinner when Mrs. Busy comes to visit?" he asked.

"*I* got something good for the dinner," answered Mrs. Miniver. "*I'm* the one who went shopping."

A little while later, a thought came to Mr. Miniver as he paid some bills in the upstairs study. "Emmie, dear," he said, "did we mail that invitation to Mrs. Busy yesterday?"

"*I* mailed the invitation, if that's what you mean," replied Mrs. Miniver.

It wasn't long before Mrs. Busy arrived for dinner. "Welcome, welcome," said Mr. Miniver, as he opened the door. "It's been so long since we drove out to see you."

"*We* drove indeed," said Mrs. Miniver, sneering. "If you recall, *I* did the driving."

Dinner proceeded and the three talked and ate and talked and talked. Mr. Miniver even managed to get in a whole sentence, short though it was. Mrs. Busy had just remarked on what a lovely place the house was, so Mr. Miniver commented, "We wanted it to look nice for you."

"And that's why *I* did all the cleaning," said Mrs. Miniver. "Honestly, Mr. M is the messiest painter on the face of the earth."

The next day when Mrs. Miniver got home from the store, Mr. Miniver was in the basement. But he had no question for his wife.

Questions about the Miniver Story

1. Is Mrs. Miniver proud? Or is she simply someone who wants an accurate description of who did what? What in the story leads you to the conclusion you have?

2. Even if you grant that Mrs. Miniver is proud, so what? What is wrong with being proud, especially when it comes from accomplishment?
3. Why does Mr. Miniver continue to say "we" as in, "Did we get something good for dinner?" or "did we mail" the invitation?
4. Should every marriage include scorekeeping so that both spouses know who is doing the most work? Discuss.

My Takeaway
Think about what you have learned. What is the most important thing you will take from this chapter? What is your "action item"?

✠
✠ ✠
Prayer
LORD, how can any of us be proud when all the good that we do and think and can ever be is a product of your Holy Spirit dwelling in us? We are deeply humbled by knowing that you have both chosen and enabled us to accomplish whatever successes can be ascribed to us. We rejoice that you, the giver of all good gifts, have allowed us to be called, not just your servants, but your children. We thank you and praise you in Jesus' name. Amen.

✠

21
House and wealth
Are an inheritance from fathers,
But a prudent wife is from the LORD
—Proverbs 19:14

Prudence, also called wisdom, was one of the four classical virtues (prudence, temperance, justice, and fortitude). A prudent wife exercises self-discipline toward her own desires, good stewardship in the use of resources, and wise judgment in general.

Husbands of women like this rejoice in their wives' circumspection, reasonableness, and practicality.

Truly, such a wife is from the Lord, a wonderful gift who smooths the road and calms the waters.

✠ ♦ ✠

Discussion Questions
1. How would you define or characterize a "prudent wife"?
2. Why is prudence important in either husband or wife or in a friend?

Word Study
Prudence: Strong's Hebrew 7919
Sakal (saw-kal')
consider, be attentive, understanding, make wise, give attention to, ponder, have insight, compre-

hend, act circumspectly, act prudently, have success, cause to prosper, teach, be intelligent, guide wisely

Prudent: **Synonyms**
sensible, level-headed, judicious, discreet, circumspect, thoughtful, reflecting, moderate, reasonable, rational, sound, using common sense, vigilant, attentive, practical, shrewd, discerning, selective, considerate, farsighted, planning ahead, prepared

Activity: The Seven Virtues

Discuss each of the following traditional virtues.
1. How can the embodiment of each virtue improve the happiness of a marriage?
2. Which of the example proverbs might serve as a behavioral habit?

Virtue	Example Proverb
Prudence	Look before you leap
Temperance	Moderation in all things
Justice	Do for others what you want them to do for you
Fortitude	Be brave
Faith	Faith is trusting God when you don't understand
Hope	God holds the future
Charity	Love your neighbor as yourself

Group Activity

In groups of 5 to 7, with a mixture of married and single people, if possible, discuss the old saying, "Most young women would rather be cute than smart because they know that most young men can see better than they can think." Is it completely silly? Insulting to one or both sexes? Partly true?

Next, follow the five steps below.

1. Have your group develop a list of what appear to be the five most important attributes men and women want in a spouse when they are still single and "shopping."
2. Rank the list from most to least important.
3. Next, using your wisdom from long experience or observation, develop a list of the five truly most important attributes that men and women should seek in a spouse that are most likely to result in a happy marriage.
4. Rank the list from most to least important.
5. Compare the lists. What do young people need to know that older married people have learned?

My Takeaway
Think about what you have learned. What is the most important thing you will take from this chapter? What is your "action item"?

✠
✠ ✠
Prayer

Our dear God, when we think about the great many blessings you have given us, and when we think about the goals we want to achieve in the future, we turn our thoughts to Solomon. When you asked him what gift he wanted from you, he did not choose wealth, power, long life, or any of the other material goods of earth. Instead, he asked for understanding, so that he might discern between good and evil and make wise choices.

LORD, we make Solomon's choice our choice and pray that you will give us deep understanding of ourselves and others, so that we, like Solomon, might gain and apply the wisdom we need to be a blessing among all those we meet. In Jesus' name we pray. Amen.

✠

22
It is better to live in a corner of the roof
Than in a house
Shared with a contentious woman.
—Proverbs 25:24

Wives who are always on their husbands about something make their husbands feel incompetent, unloved, rejected, insecure, unwanted, controlled, untrusted, and mothered. The husbands conclude that such wives now believe that their husbands are not good enough for them and regret marrying them.

Sometimes, contention in a marriage is the result of a power struggle. Before marriage, the couple did not decide who will wear the pants in the family or how the marriage will be managed. As a result, after marriage, instead of building a partnership, the couple become competitors and engage in a struggle for dominance and control.

Spouses in these marriages engage in an overt and forceful insistence on their rights, their opinions, their way of doing things, and their own standards. When one spouse doesn't follow the other's rules, a fight ensues.

Suggestions for remedying this issue:
1. Realize that you and your spouse are different people with different standards and values and tastes.
2. Realize that men and women think differently and feel differently. Assuming that

your spouse has the same perceptions and reactions that you have can cause plenty of misunderstanding.
3. Agree with your spouse that building and maintaining a loving relationship is more important than putting the cap back on the toothpaste tube, identifying who actually left the cap off, or proceeding to discuss toothpaste tubes.
4. Read Ephesians 5:1-33 together and discuss it. Is it part of the rule of your marriage?

✠ ◆ ✠

Discussion Questions
1. Of the disagreements you have with your spouse, friend, coworker, and so on, which ones are disagreements over facts, values, or personally preferred choices?
2. How important are your disagreements? Make a list of the last dozen or so disagreements and then rank them for importance on a scale of 1 to 10. Discuss how your rankings compare with your partner's.
3. Practice disagreeing with a volunteer, using the table below, first with the **Instead of** and then **Try this**. What is the difference?

Instead of	**Try this**
You're wrong	Are you sure?
That's not right	Can you clarify that for me?
I disagree	I heard a different explanation.
It isn't Jones. It's Smith.	Jones? Are you sure it wasn't Smith?

1 Corinthians 13 Checkup

In the "Love Chapter" of 1 Corinthians, Paul mentions several behaviors shown by those who love others. On page 90 is a scale for identifying the strength of those things Paul mentions.

Pair up with your spouse or a friend and work together to mark the degree of each characteristic each person has. Discuss any disagreements you find, and give examples to support your choice. However, do not get into an argument.

Total and discuss the score for each of you.

1. How similar or different are you from each other?

2. How significant do you think the results are?

3. What, if any, are the areas of disagreement over the degree of a characteristic?

4. What did you learn from this exercise?

My Takeaway

Think about what you have learned. What is the most important thing you will take from this chapter? What is your "action item"?

✠
✠ ✠

Prayer

Dear LORD, we know how hard it is to be treated harshly or to respond lovingly to a critical remark. Part of our reaction may stem from feeling unjustly accused, but part of it also comes from pride. Help us always to investigate the criticisms and disagreements aimed at us and to learn, grow, and mature from the process. We thank you that the true nature of who we are is known to you, and we pray that you will continue to mold and shape us to your service, honor, and glory. In Jesus' name. Amen.

✠

Personal Characteristics Scale from 1 Corinthians 13

is patient — is impatient

is kind — is mean

is contented — envies

is not self-centered — is an egotistical braggart

is humble — is arrogant

takes responsibility — blames others

defers to others — insists on his or her own way

is slow to get upset — is quick tempered

is accepting — is resentful

forgives and forgets wrongs — holds grudges

tells the truth — tells lies

bears adversity well — whines

trusts — distrusts

is hopeful in everything — is pessimistic

perseveres through trials — gives up

Personal Characteristics Scale from 1 Corinthians 13

is patient | is impatient

is kind | is mean

is contented | envies

is not self-centered | is an egotistical braggart

is humble | is arrogant

takes responsibility | blames others

defers to others | insists on his or her own way

is slow to get upset | is quick tempered

is accepting | is resentful

forgives and forgets wrongs | holds grudges

tells the truth | tells lies

bears adversity well | whines

trusts | distrusts

is hopeful in everything | is pessimistic

perseveres through trials | gives up

23
An angry man stirs up strife,
And a hot-tempered man
Abounds in transgression.
—Proverbs 29:22

It's one thing to be angry, but another to act it out. Acting out anger is a choice, as anyone knows who has been in the middle of a blazing argument when the phone rings. The red-faced screamer suddenly becomes calm and polite to the caller.

So, point number one: No matter how angry you are, remain calm and polite and don't act out your emotions. Let your reason prevail and discuss the issue rationally, without hurtful tones of voice or nasty comments.

Point number two, for men especially: Your wife knows that you are probably much stronger than she is physically, and anger and violence are associated together (who would have guessed?). So when you start fuming, your wife can easily become very frightened, fearful that you might hurt her. Is it worth making the woman who loves you feel afraid of being harmed, just so you can externalize your feelings?

Point number three. Angry arguments tend to escalate, as one partner sends a verbal missile one way and the other partner sends a slightly larger (louder, longer, more hurtful) one back. This continues until nuclear war happens, unless something breaks the pattern (or someone breaks something expensive).

A great example of how the escalation can be broken comes from one wife, who, when she sensed the argument was going out of control, would suddenly stick out her tongue at her husband, causing them both to start laughing. This action allowed a time out in the argument that allowed emotions to cool and reason to take over.

Point number four. Some people say really stupid things when they are raging at their spouse, things they really don't mean but things that cause hurt that will be remembered for a long time. Even if your spouse knows that what you said was preposterous, he or she will remember that the reason you said it was to cause emotional hurt. Expressing regret, repentance, and apology will help some, but the memory remains.

If you are prone to angry insults, memorize a few proverbs that can remind you to think before you speak:

- ✠ You can't unfry an egg.
- ✠ You can't unthrow a dart.
- ✠ You can't unshoot an arrow.

✠ ♦ ✠

Discussion Questions
1. "Self-control is the key to successful interpersonal relationships." Do you agree or disagree? Why?

2. Why do some people get angry over what seems to be a minor issue to others?
3. What makes you angry? How do you handle it? Is your solution a successful one?
4. If anger is a choice (as we see how easily many people can turn it off when the phone rings or someone else enters the room), why do people act it out?

Scripture Reference

"The good man brings out of his good treasure what is good; and the evil man brings out of his evil treasure what is evil. But I tell you that every careless word that people speak, they shall give an accounting for it in the day of judgment. For by your words you will be justified, and by your words you will be condemned."

—Matthew 12:35-37

My Takeaway

Think about what you have learned. What is the most important thing you will take from this chapter? What is your "action item"?

PRAYER

LORD, we come to you embarrassed to admit how easily we lose our temper, and often over the slightest things. Help us remember that we are adults in a permanent relationship, not selfish children trying to rule the playground for an afternoon. Remind us, too, that happy relationships need positive, caring, loving behaviors to keep them lasting and fulfilled. Tenderize our hearts, dear LORD, and may we always show others the love you show us. In Jesus' name. Amen.

24
*A constant dripping on a day of steady rain
And a contentious woman are alike.*
—Proverbs 27:15

The problem of contentiousness has been discussed already. But the analogy in this proverb bears a brief comment.

Once a husband gets the idea that he needs to attend to something, he's usually good to go. If his wife continues to discuss the situation after he has agreed to handle it, he feels demeaned, devalued, and humiliated, because the "lecture" his wife is giving him feels like punishment—like torture from a constant dripping.

Now, the wife might not intend her words to be received this way because she is just exploring her feelings and thinking about the issue aloud. Or she might think she is helping her husband with her comments, supplying context and details. But, and this is a difference in male and female temperaments, that's not the message the husband receives.

Note how Tom misinterprets Jane's comments in the following vignette:

Jane: Tom, the downstairs toilet keeps leaking. Could you take a look at it?
Tom: Sure, darling, right after dinner.
Jane: It's important not to have a leak in the toilet because that can waste a lot of water and raise

our water bills. And we also want to remember that water is an increasingly scarce resource. It's good environmentally to be sure that water isn't wasted by leaks. The water bill always has an insert about saving precious water and saying that leaks, especially in toilets, are a main cause of water waste in homes. Our water bill last month was $61. I wonder how much of that was due to the toilet leak?

Tom (angrily): I said I'd fix it after dinner. What do you want from me, anyway?

Sometimes, husbands think their wives are being contentious and expressing doubt about the husband's competence when the wife is simply asking questions to learn more. Example:

Sam: I'm going to ask Frank for a promotion.
Sally: Do you think you qualify?
Sam (irritated): Yes, why do you doubt me?
Sally: I don't doubt you. I just wondered what you have accomplished that merits a promotion.
Sam (blowing his cool): You have no idea how much work I put in at the office.
Sally (starting to get upset at Sam's tone): You're right, I don't. You don't talk much about what you do. How am I supposed to know?

✠ ◆ ✠

Discussion Questions

1. Marriage counselors have said that in many marriages, wives use contentiousness to gain and

maintain emotional control over the marriage. What is your response to this idea?
2. If Tom and Sam in the vignettes in this chapter felt more emotionally secure and supported by their wives, do you think these husbands would respond differently to their wives?
3. How would different tones of voice affect the way Tom and Sam received the comments by their wives?

Thought for Discussion
Many hurt feelings can be avoided if the spouses will

- state calmly and as clearly as possible what their point is
- summarize the other spouse's point before proceeding
- find areas of agreement as quickly as possible
- keep their egos in check

Scripture
"My dear friends, as a follower of our Lord Jesus Christ, I beg you to get along with each other. Don't take sides. Always try to agree in what you think."
—1 Corinthians 1:10 (CEV)

You be the Counselor
Counsel this couple:
> Dale: *"It turned out to be a bit cloudy today."*
> Loren: *"No it isn't. There's way more blue sky than clouds."*
> Dale: *"Look how crowded the sidewalks are. People are really jammed."*
> Loren: *"That's not crowded. That's nothing compared to the Walking Street last Christmas."*

> Dale: "Maybe I should stop and get gas, in case we decide to drive farther than Willets."
>
> Loren: "There's no need to stop. You've got a quarter of a tank. That's plenty."
>
> Dale: "Shall we stop at the Golden Waffle? I love their breakfasts."
>
> Loren: "I hate that place. Go to the Supreme Pancake House."
>
> Dale: "Okay. I'll just turn here."
>
> Loren: "Where do you think you're going? The way to the restaurant is to go down 4th Street."

My Takeaway

Think about what you have learned. What is the most important thing you will take from this chapter? What is your "action item"?

✠
✠ ✠

PRAYER

Dear LORD, you know we have enough criticisms and complaints in our lives. Help us to separate the valid from the invalid so that we can work on whatever needs attention. And help us as complainers to reduce the amount of negativity that we pour into our professional and family lives. We thank you and praise you for who you are and for what you bless us with. In Jesus' name. Amen.

✠

> 25
> *An excellent wife, who can find?*
> *For her worth is far above jewels.*
> *The heart of her husband trusts in her,*
> *And he will have no lack of gain.*
> *She does him good and not evil*
> *All the days of her life.*
> —Proverbs 31:10-12

Those familiar with the Bible will recognize Proverbs 31:10-31 as a key descriptor of an excellent wife. In these verses we find that the excellent wife is trustworthy, moral, happy and content, energetic, intelligent, healthy, hardworking , generous and compassionate, brave, skilled, enterprising, wise, kind, active, and faithful to God.

Of all these attributes, being faithful to God is, of course, the most important, but hard on its heels is the first one, trust. Every relationship stands or falls depending on the level of trust in it. If you cannot trust your spouse, you don't have a real relationship. You might have a transactional arrangement—you do this and I'll do that—but not a relationship. The more trust you have, the stronger your relationship will be.

Trust is the foundation of confidence, safety, security, and comfortableness in a relationship. If you want a good relationship, work to build trust and don't do anything that will reduce it. Be a brick, as they say in England — a solid, reliable partner who can be counted on.

✠ ◆ ✠

Discussion Questions
1. Why is trust so foundational to a strong relationship?
2. How does trust (in your child, your spouse, God, colleagues, new friends) grow over time? What causes trust to increase or decrease?
3. How and why are faith and trust interconnected?
4. In the table below, explain how the characteristics of trust make relationships easier, more solid, and longer lasting.
5. In the table below, explain how the characteristics that put pressure on trust slow down and reduce the quality of relationships.

Synonyms for Trust	Antonyms for Trust
confidence	distrust
faith	mistrust
assurance	suspect
credibility	doubt
reliance	wariness
sureness	misgiving
count on	qualms
rely on	disbelief

Scripture and Group Discussion
"Then the LORD God said, 'It is not good for the man to be alone; I will make him a helper suitable for him.'" — Genesis 2:18

Go to the section on Husbands in Appendix 6: The Fundamental Needs of Husbands and Wives. How well (if at all) does the description in Genesis of Eve's purpose (Genesis 2:18-24) match the stated needs of husbands (Conjugation, Cooking, and Confidence—also known as "Sex, Sandwiches, and Support") in the Appendix?

My Takeaway
Think about what you have learned. What is the most important thing you will take from this chapter? What is your "action item"?

✠
✠ ✠
Prayer

Dear LORD, thank you for being the God we can trust, knowing that what you say is true and will come to pass. Thank you for helping us to strive to be people of integrity, trustworthy in our relationships. We rejoice in the "Proverbs 31 woman," who, we see, is empowered by the trust she has earned. May we all work toward the highest standards of trust—in honesty, dependability, and faithfulness, knowing that these qualities are not only required components of Christian faith and life, but they are absolutely essential qualities to have in order for relationships to work well and be happy.

Eagerly anticipating the joy of Jesus, we pray in his name. Amen.

✠

26
Watch over your heart with all diligence,
For from it flow the springs of life.
—Proverbs 4:23

When young people want to decide on whom to date once, an important reason is often, "Well, she's beautiful," or, "Well, he's cute."

When they want to go steady, the reason changes to, "Well, she has a fun personality," or, "Well, he's funny and interesting."

But when they want to get married, the reason for their choice focuses on, "Well, she is such a good hearted girl," or, "Well, he has a kind heart."

Hence this proverb about keeping an eye on your heart. Watching over your heart means not only keeping it safe from foolish, indulgent whims, but taking care to nurture it in such a way that it can indeed become the source of the springs of life for those you meet only once, for those you become friends with, and for the person you marry.

✠ ♦ ✠

Discussion Questions
1. What are some of the problems that can be created by not diligently watching over your heart?
2. What if you give your heart away too quickly?

3. What if you hold back and avoid giving your heart even after "due diligence"?
4. What are some of the characteristics you value in a relationship that you might overlook if you weren't carefully thoughtful?
5. Thinking about the various dimensions of a relationship (intellectual, spiritual, emotional, physical, practical), which dimensions tend to get ignored in the beginning of a relationship, and which perhaps overemphasized?

You Be the Counselor

Counsel this couple. Include advice about guarding your heart and controlling your imagination:

Counselor: "So, Becky and Tim, have you had any disagreements so far?"

Tim: "No, Becky is so wonderful that she just naturally agrees with me."

Becky: "That's right. We're so wonderfully suited for each other that Tim always lets me have my way."

Counselor: "How long have you two been dating?"

Becky: "Three dreamy months." [looks at Tim with loving eyes.]

Tim: "Yeah. We've decided that we're ready to get married."

Becky: "And disagreements don't matter. Love conquers all."

Tim: "That's right. If we have a disagreement, we will just talk about it and pray about it and love each other and everything will be okay."

Counselor: "Have you discussed careers, or future education or finances, or where you want to live, or whether and when to have children?"

> *Becky: "No, that's not important as long as we have each other."*
> *Tim: "Yeah. We'll save those things for after the honeymoon."*

Scriptures for Discussion

1. Read the following passages from Ephesians and discuss their meaning and relevance to the marital relationship.
    - Ephesians 4:1-3
    - Ephesians 4:14-16
    - Ephesians 4:25, 31-32

My Takeaway

Think about what you have learned. What is the most important thing you will take from this chapter? What is your "action item"?

✠
✠ ✠

PRAYER

Dear LORD, you know how, especially in romantic relationships, we are tempted so often to throw caution to the wind and, as the songs always say, listen to our hearts instead of our heads. Help us instead to use our heads to be watchful over our hearts, knowing that our choices will have a lifelong impact on our future happiness and service to you. Send us your Holy Spirit to inform us and guide our thinking, that we may be wise, faithful, and true to our calling as your children. Thank you very much for being with our every thought and decision. In Jesus' name we pray. Amen.

✠

27
Put away from you a deceitful mouth,
And put devious lips far from you.
—Proverbs 4:24

Every relationship—whether it's one of friendship, a coworker, business to business, or marriage—begins with a token amount of trust given by each side to the other. After that, trust is gained slowly by earning it, by demonstrating that the partner in the relationship is trustworthy.

Unfortunately, there is so much untrustworthiness in modern life that trust itself has become tentative much longer than it used to be. Moreover, it is more fragile than ever before.

Hence this proverb applies powerfully to marriage. Lies and deceit can cause severe damage to a relationship—damage that can take longer to repair than you might imagine. In the area of deceit, once we find out that our trusted partner has lied or deceived even one time, we naturally wonder how many other times we have been fooled.

Think about the following scenario. Norman, afraid of getting into an argument if he were to be honest, chooses a simple lie.

Norman and his coworker Kristin were working on the Simpkins account together when lunch time arrived. So that they would not lose momen-

tum, and still have the opportunity to get away from the office, they decided to go to lunch at a local grill.

That evening, when Norman got home, his wife asked him what he did for lunch that day. Not wanting to cause his wife any jealous feelings, he decided on a convenient deception and said, "Tom and I went to lunch at a nearby coffee shop."

Unfortunately, an acquaintance of Norman and his wife had seen Norman at the grill with "another woman" and had called Norman's wife that day. Now, no matter how much apologizing, explaining, and back pedaling Norman does, his wife's trust in him has been damaged.

✠ ♦ ✠

Discussion Questions
1. How does the incident in the Garden of Eden reflect a breach of trust?
2. Do you agree that trust has become more tentative and more fragile than it used to be? Why or why not?
3. What are some ways that trust is earned?
4. Once trust is damaged, how can it be regained?

Proverb for Discussion
"O, what a tangled web we weave
When first we practice to deceive."
—Sir Walter Scott

Scripture Reference
"Then that lawless one will be revealed whom the Lord will slay with the breath of His mouth and bring to an end by the appearance of His coming;

that is, the one whose coming is in accord with the activity of Satan, with all power and signs and false wonders, and with all the deception of wickedness for those who perish, because they did not receive the love of the truth so as to be saved. For this reason God will send upon them a deluding influence so that they will believe what is false, in order that they all may be judged who did not believe the truth, but took pleasure in wickedness."
—2 Thessalonians 2:8-12

Group Discussion

Eighteenth century English writer Samuel Johnson and others have noted that deceit is worse than robbery because in a robbery the criminal is not trying to fool you about the transaction. "Give me your money or I will shoot you" is a straightforward proposition.

But if a con artist says, "Give me your money and I will invest it for you," and then steals the money, he not only has robbed you of your money, but he has weakened the bonds of trust that hold society together. You learn that you can never really trust others with the same ease that you did before.

Now move the scenario to a marital relationship.

Abe: "Honey, we're $200 short this month. Did you spend an extra $200 on something?"

Bee: "Why, no. I didn't."

When Abe finds out that Bee has indeed spent the money, Abe will be very hurt to think that Bee not only committed the offense and blew a hole in their budget, but he lied about it. Abe thinks, "Bee must take me for a fool, maintaining the lie. That's a new offense. I'll never be able to trust Bee again."

In more than one case, spouses betrayed by adultery have said that the lying denial by the guilty spouse was worse than the actual infidelity.

1. Discuss the devastating effects that any kind of deceit can have on a relationship.
2. Discuss the saying, "Love is built on trust, and trust is built on truth."

> **The Voice of Experience Reprised**
> Recently, a 90-year-old widow was asked, "What was the most important and the most powerful lesson you have learned about making a marriage successful?"
> The widow answered, **"Always tell the truth."**

My Takeaway
Think about what you have learned. What is the most important thing you will take from this chapter? What is your "action item"?

✠
✠ ✠

Prayer
Dear LORD, we ask you to impress on us again the absolute necessity for us to be frank, truthful, and straightforward in all of our interpersonal relationships, most especially in those of permanent commitment. Help us to be worthy of trust and confidence so that by modeling the highest degree of integrity we may enjoy those quietly confident relationships that only the trustworthy can possess.

We pray this in the name of the Savior Jesus, whom we can always look up to for an ideal example. Amen.

✠

28

When there are many words,
Transgression is unavoidable,
But he who restrains his lips is wise.
—Proverbs 10:19

I know what you're thinking. You think I'm going to use this as advice to women not to talk so much. You are wrong.

Women talk to see what they think and to understand how they feel. Talk is therapy for them. But when they explore their feelings and frustrations with their husbands as the audience, the husband often wants to jump in and solve the problem by giving unwanted advice.

The fact is, when a woman actually wants advice, she uses the same secret code phrase men do when they want advice: "What do you think I should do?"

So the proverb tells us not only to "Think before you speak," but for husbands to listen attentively—and quietly—when their wives are venting.

✠ ♦ ✠

Additional Proverbs

"The one who guards his mouth preserves his life; The one who opens wide his lips comes to ruin." —Proverbs 13:3

"He who restrains his words has knowledge, And he who has a cool spirit is a man of understanding." —Proverbs 17:27

"He who guards his mouth and his tongue, Guards his soul from troubles." —Proverbs 21:23

"Do you see a man who is hasty in his words? There is more hope for a fool than for him." —Proverbs 29:20

Discussion Questions

1. Why do you think there are so many bits of wisdom that recommend verbal restraint rather than speaking your mind?
    - "More have repented speech than silence."
    - "Better to remain silent and have people think you don't know anything, than to speak up and remove all doubt."
    - "Words can be explained and qualified and apologized for, but they can never be unsaid."
    - "The less said, the better."
    - "Many verbal branches means little fruit."
2. Think about the last few times someone talked a blue streak to you. What did you sense was the reason for that?

    a. the talker thought that a lot detail was needed for understanding

    b. the talker was engaging in self-justification

    c. the talker was apologizing at length

    d. the talker was attempting to persuade you to do something you didn't want to do

    e. the talker was egotistically focusing on the details of his or her life

    f. the talker is just a natural motormouth
3. What can you conclude from the reasons given to Question 2?
4. It is said that the verbal differences between men and women cause men to tune out when a woman is delivering a nonstop monologue. How can women construct their talking to men so that men can remain attentive and interested?

Idea for Comment

While most relationship counselors follow the "talk it out" philosophy for resolving issues, some counselors say that to stay happy couples should not talk about their conflicts. The idea is that each person has a different perspective on the issue and no solution is possible where each person understands the reality and facts of the situation differently. A discussion then involves a disagreement over what actually happened, what was said, what the motivation was, what the actual facts were. The more words spoken, the more disagreement and self-justification (defensiveness) and the more upset each becomes with the other. Comments?

Group Discussion

Several relationship experts have noted that a most powerful way to build a relationship is to stop talking and ask questions. At least half of a person's speaking turns must embody open-ended questions (questions that cannot be answered by a single word or phrase).
1. In your experience engaging in relationship building, how accurate do you think this is?
2. What can you say (politely and gently) to someone who talks all of the time, whether to a new or old friend?

3. Call center workers are sometimes trained to stop a constant talker by grabbing onto a piece of the talker's sentence and interrupting the talker with a comment relevant to it. Discuss how effective you think this can be. See the example below:

> *Talker: "… and then we went to Paris and saw the Eiffel Tower and I said it reminds me of the tall buildings in Chicago and – "*
> *Call Center: " – Chicago? I love Chicago, except for the winter. Let's see, you wanted your order status and, etc."*

My Takeaway
Think about what you have learned. What is the most important thing you will take from this chapter? What is your "action item"?

✠
✠ ✠
Prayer
Dear LORD, we know that a few good and sincere words, in ordinary conversation or in prayer, are better than many words that often simply make our brains lose focus. And we know that the Bible says, "Let your words be few" when praying. Let us therefore remember to be brief and to the point when speaking both to you and to your creatures, our brothers and sisters. Thank you so very much in Jesus' name. Amen.[4]

---

[4] In addition to the references in Proverbs mentioned above, see Ecclesiastes 5:3, 5:7, 6:11; Matthew 6:11.

29
Commit your works to the LORD
And your plans will be established.
— Proverbs 16:3

This final entry from the book of Proverbs reminds us that putting God at the center of your marriage and seeking his will and guidance will provide the foundation and operational wisdom for a solid, satisfying life together.

Seek God prayerfully in every decision, and commit the efforts of your marital partnership — your team — to his service (and not, by the way, to the individual self-indulgence of either of you), and your marriage will be blessed.

✠ ◆ ✠

Discussion Questions
1. How does remembering that we live and work for the Lord change the way we think and act toward each other?
2. Think of a situation or decision you have made in the past or are in the process of making. What would be the difference between approaching it in terms of either convincing your spouse or partner to agree with your viewpoint and or seeking together God's will in the decision?
3. How does your relationship with your spouse or partner need to change in order for you to

"'commit your works to the Lord" in a trusting, relaxed, confident way?

Scripture for Discussion
"Whatever you do, do your work heartily, as for the Lord rather than for men, knowing that from the Lord you will receive the reward of the inheritance. It is the Lord Christ whom you serve."
—Colossians 3:23-24

My Takeaway
Think about what you have learned. What is the most important thing you will take from this chapter? What is your "action item"?

✠
✠ ✠

Prayer
Lord God, it sometimes seems that when we pray or think about spiritual things, we are always saying the words, "I," "me," "my," and "mine," instead of "you," "your," and "yours." We always need your help, yet our hearts are out of focus, and we want you to solve our problems in the way we have designed. Instead, help us to remember your Godly sovereignty and let us focus on serving you with all our energy. Remind us that the prayer Jesus gave us to use includes, "*May your will be done, on earth as it is in heaven.*"

We thank you in Jesus' name. Amen.

✠

30
Nevertheless let each individual among you
Also love his own wife even as himself;
And let the wife see to it that she
Respect her husband.
—Ephesians 5:33

Of all the verses in the Bible on marriage outside of the book of Proverbs, this one encapsulates the path to marital happiness more completely than any other. Rightly understood and rightly applied, this Scripture would bring happiness and contentment to a large percentage of troubled marriages.

Husbands: Love your wives. Love is singled out in this Scripture for men to give to their wives in part because wives need regular, or even frequent, reassurance that they are loved. Let them know that you care about them. Listen to them when they need to talk (and don't offer solutions, just listen). Show your wife some affection. Tell her you appreciate her. Tell her that you are glad you married her.

Wives: Respect your husbands. Respect is singled out in this Scripture for wives to give to their husbands because disrespect is the most hurtful and damaging attitude a wife can display toward her husband. Never roll your eyes in contempt, don't criticize, don't correct your husband publicly. When you disagree (privately), put your disagreement in the form of a question. That is, instead of saying, "You're wrong. It was Joe Green who said that, not Ted Brown," ask, "Wasn't it Joe Green who said that?" or "Ted Brown? I thought it was Joe Green."

Husbands: Love involves communicating with your wife, and making her feel secure and safe. Get to know your wife and open up to her so that she can know you. As Brother Lawrence says in *The Practice of the Presence of God*, "We must know before we can love" (Ninth Letter), and, "As knowledge is commonly the measure of love, the deeper and wider our knowledge, the greater will be our love" (Sixteenth Letter).

Wives: Respect involves giving your husband the benefit of the doubt, trusting him, cutting him some slack, and forgiving him. And none of this, "You're perfect, now change," stuff. The only way to change your husband is to change yourself.

Husbands: Remember that love is a verb — an action. The action can be small, such as a loving note where she will find it in the course of the day, but it should be clear enough to get the message across and for your wife to tell other women.

Wives: Remember that respect is conveyed by your tone of voice and your facial expression as well as your words.

When a husband shows love for his wife, she also feels respected; when a wife shows respect for her husband, he also feels loved.

✠ ◆ ✠

Discussion Questions

1. It has been said that *love* has more different meanings than almost any other word in the English language. Think about what is meant by the following expressions. What do these uses of *love* have in common? What does *love* mean?
   - I love coffee ice cream
   - I love my dog
   - I love action adventure movies
   - I love a good joke
   - I love my children
   - I love Saturday afternoons

2. Moreover, when people tell each other that they love one another, while they might think they know what the other person means, they are quite possibly in error. So the next questions are:
   - How would you define *love* between a husband and a wife?
   - Is there a difference between the love that two people feel when romantically attached or newly married and the love that a husband and wife feel when they have been married for many years?

3. So then, what does Paul mean when he commands husbands to love their wives?

4. Why is it important for a husband to love his wife?
5. What are some behaviors that show that a wife respects her husband?
6. What are some behaviors that show that a wife does not respect her husband?
7. Why is it important for wives to respect their husbands? Or, why do you think Paul didn't just tell wives to love their husbands, as he tells husbands to love their wives?
8. How do love and respect mesh with each partner's role in a marriage?

Quotation for Discussion
"Love means respecting your wife's partnership; respect means loving your husband's leadership."
—Proverb

You Be the Counselor
1. In your experience, what causes husbands to stop expressing love for their wives?
2. What causes some wives to stop showing respect for their husbands?
3. What would Paul—or God, who inspired Paul—say to the idea that the Scripture says, "Husbands, love your wives *unless* . . ." or "Wives, respect your husbands *unless* . . ."

Love of the Wife
Return to Appendix 6, "The Fundamental Needs of Husbands and Wives in Marriage," and read once again the section, Wives.
1. What are some things suggested in the section Love and Emotional Connection that husbands can use to show their love for their wives?
2. What are some ideas for demonstrating love for your spouse suggested by the entire section?

My Takeaway
Think about what you have learned. What is the most important thing you will take from this chapter? What is your "action item"?

☦
☦ ☦
Prayer

Dear God, we know that the formula for a happy and prosperous marriage is so simple. And yet why do we so imperfectly put it into practice? Help us, LORD, to fight against the temptations to be critical, negative, disrespectful, and especially contemptuous. For we know that those expressions do not come from a loving place and they should not be welcome in our relationships. Strengthen us to become conquerors in this battle, a battle that must be fought with the weapons of kindness, encouragement, support, and affection. In Jesus' name we ask. Amen.

☦

Part Two
Proverbs from Elsewhere

31
A cheerful look makes a dish a feast.
—English Proverb[5]

This proverb gets at the heart of a successful marriage. A happy wife makes a husband feel loved and respected. A happy husband makes a wife feel safe and secure. Expressing your happiness — or at least contentment — will reassure your spouse. It's especially important to do this at mealtime.

You aren't always going to be happy when it's time to eat, of course, either because of the events of your day or the events of your spouse's day. But if you put on a cheerful face and a kind, warm tone of voice, you'll not only make the dining experience more pleasant for those around you, but you might find that you are beginning to feel more cheerful, too.

And, if need be, after you enjoy the meal in peace and harmony, and allow your food and your thoughts to digest and settle, you can then discuss whatever issues need to be discussed — away from the table.

☦

Let all bitterness and wrath and anger and clamor and slander be put away from you, along with all malice. Be kind to one another,

---

[5] George Herbert, *Outlandish Proverbs*. London: Humphrey Bluden, 1640. Proverb 62. Spelling modernized.

tender-hearted, forgiving each other, just as God in Christ also has forgiven you.
    —*Ephesians 4:31-32*

✠ ♦ ✠

Discussion Questions
1. When you first meet someone, are you more attracted to a welcoming smile or a deeply thoughtful scowl?
2. What first attracted you to the person you eventually married? Did happiness (smiling, laughter, fun) play a role? Explain.
3. How does the Biblical injunction to be kind to one another (Ephesians 4:31-32) influence the way you interact with other Christians? If you have not yet come to the Lord, how would this command affect the way you behave toward others?
4. A social counselor once remarked that each of us has an obligation to act happy around others, even if we are not happy, because showing our discontent is self-indulgent and offensive. What do you think? If you act unhappy in public, is that just a selfish attempt to get attention?

Quotations for Discussion
"There are many pains and sorrows in this life, but to call attention to the ones we ourselves now face is needlessly to diminish the modicum of happiness enjoyed by others." —Unknown

"If women knew the power of a smile, they would quickly rule the world." —Anonymous

"Good humor may be defined as a habit of being pleased; a constant and perennial softness of manner, easiness of approach, and suavity[6] of disposition." —Samuel Johnson, Rambler 72

My Takeaway
Think about what you have learned. What is the most important thing you will take from this chapter? What is your "action item"?

✠ ✠
Prayer
LORD, thank you so much for the gift of happiness, of laughter, of smiles, of cheerful looks, for the great, peaceful feeling of contentment, joyfulness, and bliss. We so deeply and thoroughly enjoy these experiences that we ask you to make us your instruments for bringing such moments to others. How happy it will make us if we can give happiness to those who need it.

Dear LORD, please give us the opportunities, the specific appointments, together with the right words and the right deeds that we might increase the joy of the world even a little—perhaps one person at a time. In Jesus' name. Amen.

✠

---

[6] Suavity: charmingly courteous, making one feel relaxed and comfortable.

32
A husband is not a project.
— Angela Birch

Overheard in a restaurant: "He's really a nice guy. After we're married, there are only five things I want to change about him."

An attitude and expectation like this, of course, will result in a very stressful and unhappy marriage. Men do not want to be mothered (except when they are sick and their wives make lots of chicken soup for them). A man wants to feel competent and accepted. If he feels that his wife is always trying to fix him, he will feel broken and rejected.

Wives and husbands should both understand that they can't change each other. Others have to want to change themselves. The only person you can change is yourself. But if you do change yourself, into a model that your spouse can treasure and enjoy, you'll soon discover that your spouse has chosen to change, too.

☩

Is there any encouragement from belonging to Christ? Any comfort from His love? Any fellowship together in the Spirit? Are your hearts tender and compassionate? Then make me truly happy by agreeing wholeheartedly with each other, loving one another, and working together with one mind and purpose. Don't be

selfish; don't try to impress others. Be humble, thinking of others as better than yourselves. Don't look out only for your own interests, but take an interest in others, too.
—*Philippians 2:1-4 (NLT)*

✠ ♦ ✠

Discussion Questions
1. Why does the proverb say, "a husband," rather than "a wife" or "a spouse"?
2. If a wife should not take on changing her husband in some area as a "project," what *should* she do if she is irritated by one or more of her husband's shortcomings?
3. How does "changing yourself to change your spouse" work? How can both husbands and wives, and people in close friendship, profit from this advice?

Quotation for Discussion
"The companion of an evening and the companion for life require very different qualifications."
—Samuel Johnson

Scriptures for Discussion
"Finally, brethren, rejoice, be made complete, be comforted, be like-minded, live in peace; and the God of love and peace will be with you."
—2 Corinthians 13:11

"Therefore, accept one another, just as Christ also accepted us to the glory of God."
—Romans 15:17

You Be the Counselor
What advice or counsel would you give to the young woman quoted earlier, who said, "There are only five things I want to change about him"?

Additional Commentary
Wives who view their husbands as projects with areas of needed improvement not only discover the cost and difficulty of changing anything about their spouses, but they also tend to adopt the belief that there is always something wrong with him and that therefore their project is a lifetime effort. Imagine how a husband feels when he understands that his wife thinks he is so faulty and incompetent that she plans to spend the rest of her life trying to repair his defects.

Newly minted husbands are often shocked to find out that their brides have changed the music from "You're perfect" to "It's time for a change." Another reason for husbands' concern is that most of them do not have a checklist of their wives' defects for their wives to address. This causes them to think, "I'm the only defective person here?"

Objection, Your Honor
But what if you really insist on trying to change some of your husband's obviously irritating behaviors? Here are some ideas to think about, to minimize the likelihood of estrangement or divorce from your spouse.

1. **Is the behavior changeable** or is it part of your spouse's permanent personality? It's quite unlikely to change a shy person into a life-of-the-party extrovert. A hypersensitive person can probably not be refashioned into a nothing-bothers-me image-of-steel fighter aircraft test pilot type.

2. **How important is it to make the change?** Does the behavior have serious implications for the marriage? Or are you being ridiculously picky? For example, if your spouse says things such as, "We haven't went there yet, but her and I are planning to go soon," the glaringly incorrect grammar is likely to create the image of an uneducated, unintelligent person, whose prospects for promotion at work are diminished. Such a situation impacts the marriage and is worth addressing. On the other hand, if your spouse is in the habit of piling his shoes on top of each other to "save space," perhaps you should see it in the broader context of your marriage and just learn to ignore it.
3. **Is it worth the cost?** Every attempt to change a person's habit or behavior comes at a cost to the relationship. Depending on the change you want and how difficult it is, the cost might be that your husband (or wife) shares feelings less, offers more careful responses to questions (the walking on eggshells defense mechanism), and always feels on edge or less relaxed. Or your partner is simply not very happy.
4. **Are you merely trying to establish or maintain control over your spouse?** In situations like this, your husband-as-a-project quickly becomes an emotional target, where you always have something to criticize in order to maintain your position of superiority. A life of hectoring your husband will make him miserable. Is that your goal?
5. **Who decided that making this change is important?** Did you get together with your spouse, discuss the issue, and both agree that a change of the kind and in the direction you had in mind is important? Or are you planning to

impose your required change on your spouse without discussion or agreement, just by criticizing and nagging?

6. **Have you discussed the issue with your spouse and agreed on *who* should change?** Perhaps the solution to your irritation lies not in your spouse's changing, but in your changing. For example, a common complaint by wives is that their husbands can't remember to put the toilet seat down when they are finished. Why not solve the problem by agreeing that both of you should always expect the seat to be in the up position? Or that both the seat and the lid should always be closed?

7. **What will you change while your spouse is changing?** Ask your spouse what behaviors he or she would like you to change while you both work on the change you want. This practice will make the marriage a team project for improving the marriage itself rather than just one partner.

Objection Activity

On the following page is a worksheet with several sample irritants that husbands often cause their wives to suffer. Pair up with your spouse and fill out the worksheet together.

Key: Discuss each behavior listed below. Assign a number from 1 to 10, where 10 is most important or most possible.
HI, write the number representing the husband's view of importance of changing; WI, wife's view of importance of changing; HP, husband's view of the possibility of changing; WP, wife's view of the possibility of changing

The blanks in numbers 21 to 25 are for you and your spouse to fill in whatever behaviors you want.

When you have completed the worksheet, compare your answers and discuss any variations you have. Are there some items that the husband

Marriage in a Nutshell: Expanded Edition ✝ 133

1.	HI	WI	HP	WP	Leaves items on the vanity that should be put back into a drawer
2.	HI	WI	HP	WP	Smokes in the house
3.	HI	WI	HP	WP	emotionally distant, doesn't' share life with spouse
4.	HI	WI	HP	WP	leaves dirty laundry everywhere
5.	HI	WI	HP	WP	critical of behavior and or ideas
6.	HI	WI	HP	WP	hard to please
7.	HI	WI	HP	WP	complains of wife's bad cooking
8.	HI	WI	HP	WP	different religion
9.	HI	WI	HP	WP	watches too much TV
10.	HI	WI	HP	WP	unambitious
11.	HI	WI	HP	WP	too shy and reserved
12.	HI	WI	HP	WP	careless of personal appearance
13.	HI	WI	HP	WP	poor table manners
14.	HI	WI	HP	WP	leaves toilet seat up
15.	HI	WI	HP	WP	can never find keys when it's time to leave
16.	HI	WI	HP	WP	doesn't wipe shower glass down when finished taking a shower
17.	HI	WI	HP	WP	leaves bathroom scale out after weighing self
18.	HI	WI	HP	WP	doesn't fill the car with gas
19.	HI	WI	HP	WP	leaves dishes in the sink
20.	HI	WI	HP	WP	
21.	HI	WI	HP	WP	
22.	HI	WI	HP	WP	
23.	HI	WI	HP	WP	
24.	HI	WI	HP	WP	
25.	HI	WI	HP	WP	

should attempt to change or improve? Are there some items the wife should stop complaining about? What are each of you going to do to increase harmony, compatibility, and happiness in your marriage?

Use of the extra blank worksheets is optional.

Counting the Criticisms

Some counselors say that for every criticism aimed at a spouse, five praises, encouragements, or appreciations must be given if the balance of a positive environment, and therefore a happy marriage, is to be maintained.

1. Of the people you have known (married, engaged, dating) how many of them seem to produce a 5-to-1 ratio of compliments to criticism?
2. Do those in the 5-to-1 relationships appear to be happier than those with lower ratios?
3. Given the stress in most relationships, is a 5-to-1 relationship practical? Possible? 3to 1? 2 to 1?

My Takeaway

Think about what you have learned. What is the most important thing you will take from this chapter? What is your "action item"?

☫
☫ ☫

PRAYER

LORD, help us to realize that too often our desire to find fault and criticize others comes not from a genuine desire to improve them but from a backhanded way of feeling superior by praising ourselves. Help us to remove the plank from our own eye before we try to take a speck from our spouse's eye. Thank you for this insight. May we meditate on it. In Jesus' name. Amen.

☫

Marriage in a Nutshell: Expanded Edition ✞ 135

1.	HI	WI	HP	WP	
2.	HI	WI	HP	WP	
3.	HI	WI	HP	WP	
4.	HI	WI	HP	WP	
5.	HI	WI	HP	WP	
6.	HI	WI	HP	WP	
7.	HI	WI	HP	WP	
8.	HI	WI	HP	WP	
9.	HI	WI	HP	WP	
10.	HI	WI	HP	WP	
11.	HI	WI	HP	WP	
12.	HI	WI	HP	WP	
13.	HI	WI	HP	WP	
14.	HI	WI	HP	WP	
15.	HI	WI	HP	WP	
16.	HI	WI	HP	WP	
17.	HI	WI	HP	WP	
18.	HI	WI	HP	WP	
19.	HI	WI	HP	WP	
20.	HI	WI	HP	WP	
21.	HI	WI	HP	WP	
22.	HI	WI	HP	WP	
23.	HI	WI	HP	WP	
24.	HI	WI	HP	WP	
25.	HI	WI	HP	WP	

1.	HI	WI	HP	WP	
2.	HI	WI	HP	WP	
3.	HI	WI	HP	WP	
4.	HI	WI	HP	WP	
5.	HI	WI	HP	WP	
6.	HI	WI	HP	WP	
7.	HI	WI	HP	WP	
8.	HI	WI	HP	WP	
9.	HI	WI	HP	WP	
10.	HI	WI	HP	WP	
11.	HI	WI	HP	WP	
12.	HI	WI	HP	WP	
13.	HI	WI	HP	WP	
14.	HI	WI	HP	WP	
15.	HI	WI	HP	WP	
16.	HI	WI	HP	WP	
17.	HI	WI	HP	WP	
18.	HI	WI	HP	WP	
19.	HI	WI	HP	WP	
20.	HI	WI	HP	WP	
21.	HI	WI	HP	WP	
22.	HI	WI	HP	WP	
23.	HI	WI	HP	WP	
24.	HI	WI	HP	WP	
25.	HI	WI	HP	WP	

33
More have repented speech than silence.
—English Proverb[7]

Ever say something you regretted later? How many times? Ever regretted not saying something when you wanted to speak but didn't? How many times?

Seems as if some of us prove the proverb's accuracy. Mostly because some of us are blurters. We blurt out the first thing that comes to mind without first considering the impact or consequences on the receiver. And we blurt before listening long enough to understand the situation fully.

A good deal of repented speech comes from our bad interpersonal habits. One such habit is blaming. Instead of supporting their spouse by taking their spouse's side in an event, blamers habitually take the opposite side.

For example, one spouse comes home and says, "The boss chewed me out today for one tiny error on one spreadsheet."

The supportive spouse will say, "That's terrible. How can he be so critical when you work so hard?"

The blamer spouse will say, "Well, you ought to be more careful. Don't you check your work?"

---

[7] Herbert, Proverb 682. Spelling modernized.

Here the blamer hits the spouse with a few additional punches, showing that the blamer neither trusts nor respects the spouse. Silence would have been much better.

And now for another proverb about thinking before you speak:

> ✠ Once you throw a rock, you can't change your mind.

Love is patient, love is kind and is not jealous; love does not brag and is not arrogant, does not act unbecomingly; it does not seek its own, is not provoked, does not take into account a wrong suffered, does not rejoice in unrighteousness, but rejoices with the truth; bears all things, believes all things, hopes all things, endures all things. Love never fails. . . .
—1 Corinthians 13:4-8a

✠ ◆ ✠

Discussion Questions
1. What are the kinds of things we usually regret saying the most?
2. In the following list, which do we most regret saying and why?
    A. Praising other people.
    B. Praising (bragging about) ourselves.
    C. Criticizing other people.
    D. Criticizing ourselves.
3. Do you know anyone who is a "blamer spouse"? Does their marriage seem to be happy?
4. Do you know anyone who is a "supportive spouse"? Does their marriage appear to be suc-

cessful and happy?
5. Are you intentional in striving to be a supportive spouse? Explain.
6. Does an "occasional blamer spouse" differ from a "chronic blamer spouse"? If so, how?

Additional Commentary
Whenever one spouse reports a "bad experience" story to the other, several dynamics are set in motion.
1. Reporting the bad news represents an appeal for sympathy. The spouse who refuses to sympathize is rejecting the appeal.
2. Siding with the source of the bad experience rejects the spouse's point of view, sides with the original criticizer, and often adds a new criticism of the spouse.

Tell the Good, Silence the Bad
The more often a blamer spouse responds critically to the spouse's "bad experience" story, the less often the blamer spouse will hear such stories, meaning that there will be less bonding because of less communication.

Note that in the example here, even though the supportive spouse has little idea about the actual situation, he or she immediately joins on the side of the spouse, criticizes the spouse's boss, and reinforces trust and confidence in the spouse.

The blamer spouse, on the other hand, instead of seeking more facts and context, invents two possible reasons for the reprimand: (1) you're not being careful and (2) you must not be checking (or competently checking) your work.

Which of these spouses would you want to come home to every night?

Group Activity
Choose volunteers to read each of the following regrettable sentences aloud, using that tone of voice we are all familiar with. What would be the difference between a spouse speaking the sentence and not speaking it?

1. "That's the second plate you've broken this week. What's wrong with you, anyway?"
2. "I told you to get milk on the way home. Can't you remember anything? Now I can't make mashed potatoes. My dinner will be ruined, all thanks to you. I don't know why I try."
3. "Someone spilled glop all over the front seat of my car. And don't try to look innocent. I know you did it. My seats are real leather and this is going to be at least a $1,000 job. I suppose you are going to tell me you were trying to be careful."
4. "Look at this! Look at this! My phone has a 3 percent charge on it. Why didn't you plug it in last night? You know that's one of your simple chores. I guess they must not be so simple after all, at least not for you. Just what part of *Plug the phone in every night* don't you understand?"
5. "I can't believe you left the cover off the barbeque again. And with the rain forecast, the whole thing is likely to be ruined. And here I just got through telling Norma that you were behaving a little less like a child recently. Now I have to eat my words. So not only have you humiliated me, but you will obviously never mature into a man who can handle responsibility or be competent at anything. Hmmph. Man of the house. I wish."
6. "Where have you been? You said you would meet me at noon for lunch and it's nearly 12:30 now. Don't you know that I have to be back at

the office by 1:15? Do you think you can just show up whenever you want, while I'm under a huge time constraint? Well, this is the last time I eat lunch with you!"

You Be the Counselor
Suppose you meet a couple who behave toward each other the way the couples do in the previous group activity. Imagine that either one or both spouses talk this way. How would you counsel them?

My Takeaway
Think about what you have learned. What is the most important thing you will take from this chapter? What is your "action item"?

✠
✠ ✠
Prayer

LORD, your word reminds us that the tongue is like a sword, that can cut and slash and chop and inflict deep wounds that can last years and can sometimes only partially heal.

Please remind us that in our true and sane moments we don't want to hurt our spouse, our partner, our friend, whom we have promised to love and respect for the remainder of our lives, and who we hope and pray will forgive, love, and honor us in spite of our sometimes mean behavior.

Lastly, let us understand that expressing contempt toward our spouse dishonors Christ as it dishonors the one he has given to us, to be our companion and partner. Thank you for hearing our request. In Jesus' name. Amen.

✠

34
A good husband makes a good wife.
A good wife makes a good husband.
—English Proverbs[8]

You might have heard the parallel sayings, "Be glad about your husband's flaws, because they are what kept him from getting a better wife," and "Be glad about your wife's flaws, because they are what kept her from getting a better husband."

The point is, instead of criticizing your spouse's shortcomings, model the kind of spouse you want your partner to be and be the kind of spouse your partner would enjoy and adore.

This is another way of saying, "Instead of focusing on your spouse's flaws, focus on your own and work to repair them." That will keep you busy enough and be more effective in producing a better spouse.

✣

Let all that you do be done in love.
—1 Corinthians 16:14

✠ ♦ ✠

---

[8] Wolfgang Mieder, ed., *The Prentice-Hall Encyclopedia of World Proverbs*. 1986. Rpt., MJF Books, 1996. Proverbs 8224 and 17348.

Discussion Questions
1. If these proverbs are true, why aren't there more good husbands and good wives?
2. What are some specific examples of "goodness" to a spouse or friend that will positively impact the relationship?
3. What, do you suppose, is the process of "making a good spouse" like? How is it done?
4. We are told that because we can't change others, we should change ourselves—and that changing ourselves is the surest way to a future life of love and service. How can that concept be reconciled with these proverbs?
5. During an argument, some couples find themselves in a "downward spiral," where they play "one-upmanship," or "I can top that" by responding to each other's responses with a verbal blow harder than the previous one. As a result, the interaction becomes more and more negative. How could arguments be changed into "upward spirals," where each reply is kinder and more positive than the previous?

Group Activity
Create a list of action words that will help make a good spouse. Explain why each word you choose will be effective. (See the examples, below.)

Example Action Words
Model: modeling good or kind behavior will encourage your spouse to do the same.
Accept: accepting a few of the unpleasant things in our day will cause less stress than rejecting everything.
Help: step in and help your spouse with whatever tasks they are performing (dishes, yard work, bills, child care).

Focus on the Positive

Here's a game you can play with your spouse. Use a source of documentation to keep track of your answers (pad and paper, cell phone note app, etc.).

1. Each player writes down three things they like about their spouse. They share their answers.
2. The wife then writes one more thing (not already on the list) and shares it with her husband.
3. The husband then writes another, different thing and shares it with his wife.
4. Play continues until one player runs out of things to list and surrenders.

My Takeaway

Think about what you have learned. What is the most important thing you will take from this chapter? What is your "action item"?

✠
✠ ✠

Prayer

LORD, we know what to do to make a happy relationship—be kind and warm and supportive to our spouse. So why don't we do those things? Why does our ego and the need to be right so often get in the way of a productive discussion?

Help, us, LORD, to stop making the excuse that we are only human. Send your Spirit to us to reinforce our determination to be a good spouse and to pursue those things that will be positive and effective. May we work together as a team and not keep tripping over our pride. In Jesus' name. Amen.

✠

35
When husband and wife
Agree with each other,
They can dry up the ocean with buckets.
— Vietnamese Proverb[9]

You've heard the expression that "two working together can do the work of three working by themselves." That's the benefit of teams.

This proverb reminds us that marriage is intended to be a collaboration, a joint effort, where the spouses form a team moving and working in the same direction, toward the same goals.

Spouses who play tug-of-war with each other are going to end up frustrated and tired, with little progress to show for the effort. If they would pull in the same direction, how much farther they could get.

Remember that you are a team with your spouse. Develop common goals and work together toward them. You are not two individuals who happen to be married; you are a collaborative team that should function as a unit.

---

[9] Mieder, Proverb 8241.

✝

Two are better than one because they have a good return for their labor. For if either of them falls, the one will lift up his companion. But woe to the one who falls when there is not another to lift him up. Furthermore, if two lie down together, they keep warm, but how can one keep warm alone? And if one can overpower him who is alone, two can resist him. A cord of three strands is not quickly torn apart.
—Ecclesiastes 4:9-12

✠ ♦ ✠

Discussion Questions
1. It is sometimes said that men and women are so different from each other because that allows them to form a strong team, with more insight into the problems (and joys!) of life that two men or two women could get. What do you think and why?
2. Some married partners are convinced instead of being a team member, their spouse is simply stubborn, prideful, selfish, controlling, and independent. What are some problems and some opportunities that help or hinder spouses working together as a team?
3. If you are looking for a spouse, should your search be for someone as different from you as possible or as similar as possible? Explain why.

Group Discussion
 Husbands and wives who work together in a formal job situation sometimes find themselves at odds with each other, competing for the things they should have been working together to achieve. As a

result, their marriage is made more difficult, more stressful, and less happy.

The cause of this change from supporter to competitor has been attributed to many things, including

- the natural competitiveness of humans
- the male need for goal achievement and conquest
- the rise of feminism
- the natural opportunity to battle out personal marital issues by using workplace proxies.

Discuss this issue as a group.
- Is the phenomenon true?
- If so, what is the cause?
- And if true, how can it be avoided?

My Takeaway
Think about what you have learned. What is the most important thing you will take from this chapter? What is your "action item"?

Prayer

Dear LORD, our prayer is that you will help us in all of our relationships to live together in peace and harmony, and especially in our marriage relationship. Help us to learn how to make our teammate happy and successful so that our team can not only survive the troubles and challenges we all face, but so that we can thrive. We ask this in the name of our loving savior, Jesus. Amen.

☦

36
Do not belittle the wife;
She is the home.
— African Proverb[10]

During the course of your marriage, you might live in a one-bedroom apartment, then a two or three bedroom apartment, then a condo or townhouse, then a starter-size single family house, and eventually a two-story house with a big yard.

But each one of these living structures will be your home at the time. What is it that makes a house into a home? Yes, it's your wife. As the proverb says, your wife *is* your home.

After a long trip, you are on the flight back. What do you tell the passenger next to you? "I'm on the way home to my house" or "I'm on the way home to my wife"?

You've heard the expression, "Home is where the heart is." When you are married, that means, "Home is where your wife is."

Cherish your home.

So husbands ought also to love their own wives as their own bodies. He who loves his own wife loves himself. . . .
—Ephesians 5:28

---

[10] Mieder, Proverb 17379.

Discussion Questions
1. What does it mean to say that the wife "is the home"?
2. What things does the wife supply to the house you live in that makes it a home?
3. Can a motel or a campsite be a home? Explain.

Group Discussion
Arrange yourselves in groups of 2 to 5. Together, formulate a definition of *home*. In your discussion, include aspects of home that involve the psychological, the emotional, the spiritual, the physical, the relational, and so forth.

Reassemble as a whole and compare your definitions.

My Takeaway
Think about what you have learned. What is the most important thing you will take from this chapter? What is your "action item"?

Prayer
Dear LORD, thank you so much for the wives who strive with so much love and effort to turn four walls into a loving sanctuary where their husbands can rest comfortably and happily. May we always recognize and appreciate that the wife's love makes a home out of any dwelling place. We thank you in Jesus' name. Amen.

37
Men get the gist,
Women get the details.
— American Proverb

Men tend to remember the big picture, the general circumstances of an event, especially an interpersonal event (date, party, get together), while women remember the situation in detail.

Details that are important to a woman are often not important to a man. Note the following story, which I heard somewhere long ago.

Jim and Tim decided to go hunting one weekend. Jim stopped by Tim's house just long enough to pack Tim's gear into the pickup truck and wave goodbye to Tim's wife.

The two buddies had a great time, until about ten hours into their outing, when they were separated while stalking a deer. When Jim didn't return to the campsite by the next morning, Tim took the truck back home and reported the incident. The authorities came to interview Tim.

"What was he wearing?" one officer asked.

"Normal hunting clothes," Tim said.

"Could you be more specific?" the officer said.

"Well, I'm not sure, but I think he had on a jacket." This was as detailed as Tim could be after spending ten hours with Jim.

On the other hand, Tim's wife, who had seen Jim for all of two minutes the day before, said, "He was wearing a red, black, and white plaid jacket, a brown shirt with button pockets, blue jeans with a black belt, and brown leather mid-calf lace-up boots."

Years later, when Tim told the story to others, he would say that Jim was wearing his camouflage jacket. His wife would correct him, making him upset.

When recounting events that they have remembered only the gist or summary of, men often fill in the details with plausible specifics, if they can't remember the actual details. (They may not realize they are doing this.)

In a marriage, these discrepancies can cause a lot of misunderstanding, disagreement, and criticism by the wife, since she remembers the details. To the husband the details don't matter, but are just window dressing. To hear his wife repeatedly correct him in front of others over meaningless specifics makes him feel devalued and even insulted.

On the other hand, when specifics are important to a man, he will indeed recall the details. If we return to the story above, we will see just that.

"Was the man armed?" asked the officer.
"Yes, he had a gun," Tim's wife said.
"What kind?" the officer said.
"A rifle of some kind," she said.
"It was an Acme Model 8942 Conqueror .30 caliber modified bolt action rifle with an 8-power

KillView scope," said Tim. "There was a slight scratch on the left side of the stock."

Tim's wife didn't care about the details of Jim's rifle and so didn't pay attention to them, just as Tim didn't care about the details of Jim's clothing.

Lessons for a Happy Marriage
1. **Wives,** don't correct your husband in front of others, if at all. In casual conversation, the goal is not to establish every fact correctly; the goal is to be sociable.
2. **Husbands,** if you are in doubt about a social detail in your narrative (the date, location, and so forth), feel free to give a nod to your wife to fill in the blank. She will likely be glad to help you.

✟

. . . Walk in a manner worthy of the calling with which you have been called, with all humility and gentleness, with patience, showing forbearance to one another in love, being diligent to preserve the unity of the Spirit in the bond of peace.
—Ephesians 4:1b-3

Discussion Questions

1. It's obvious that we pay more attention to the things that interest us than we do to things that don't interest us. Could this fact help explain the perceived differences in recollection between men and women? That is, men and women differ in what interests them and this reveals itself in how many and what details each recalls in a given experience. Discuss. Offer examples.
2. Are you a chronic corrector or do you know anyone who is? Why do correctors feel the need to be exact with every detail in a story?
3. Does correcting a story improve it for the listener? If so, in what way?

Story for Discussion
Read the following story and answer the questions.

A MODERN MIRACLE

Adam: "Hey, Mel. I heard you had an exciting adventure last week."

Mel: "You bet. It was an eye opener."

Adam: "Tell me what happened."

Mel: "It was last Wednesday — "

Nell: "It was last Tuesday, Mel. Remember?"

Mel: "Oh, yes, thanks, Nell. Anyway, we were driving toward Weedville, when — "

Nell: "We had already passed Weedville, and were approaching the big, flat area that fills with water whenever it rains."

Mel: "So, my car — "

Nell: "The rental car, he means."

Mel: "Suddenly starts talking to me. I mean — "

Nell: "The voice was preceded by a beep."

> Mel: "I heard this voice, which sounded like a young man – "
>
> Nell: "The voice was that of a young woman, low, but definitely feminine."
>
> Mel: "And the voice says, 'You are low on gas.'"
>
> Nell: "Actually, the voice said, 'Fuel level is low.'"
>
> Mel: "And it said, 'Here are the closest six gas stations.'"
>
> Nell: "That's not right. The voice said, 'There are six gas stations nearby.'"
>
> Mel: "Can you believe the sophistication and personalization of technology today? I mean, it's amazing. We picked a Krengel station and got gas right away."
>
> Nell: "Well, no. We were going to a Chubfon station, but I noticed that it was on the other side of the freeway. So, I checked the map and saw a Krengel station a couple of off-ramps away and so we stopped there."
>
> Mel: "And to think about it, in the old days, we would have been stuck on the road in the middle of nowhere, with an empty gas can, and trying to thumb a ride to the nearest filling station."
>
> Nell: "In the old days, if Mel had ever run out of gas while I was with him, I never would have married him."
>
> Adam: "That is an amazing story, Mel."
>
> Mel: "Yeah. Thanks."

Questions

1. Does Nell's contribution as corrector enhance the story? If so, in what way or ways? If not, why not?
2. If you were Adam, what would you think about Nell's participation in Mel's story?

3. If you were Mel, how would you describe Nell's participation in the story?
4. If you were Nell, how would you describe your participation in the story?
5. Suppose you were Nell, and several days later you remembered that the fuel level warning voice was preceded by three beeps instead of one, and that, instead of saying, "gas stations nearby," the warning voice had said, "gas stations close to you." Should you call Adam and correct the inaccuracies in the story? Why or why not?
6. Suppose you were Nell, and Mel, instead of being your husband, is your supervisor at an electronics manufacturing company. Would you change your participation in the story in any way? Why or why not?

My Takeaway

Think about what you have learned. What is the most important thing you will take from this chapter? What is your "action item"?

✠
✠ ✠
Prayer

Lord, we know that we are flawed human beings, probably wrong more often than right. And we know that attention to details often belongs more to one spouse than to the other. And we know that sometimes details are important and sometimes not. Help us to discern the difference and to be careful in how we address the inaccuracies of others, especially in social situations. In Jesus' name we thank you. Amen.

✠

38
Income, 100; outgo, 99; result: happiness.
Income, 100; outgo, 101; result: misery.
— After an English Proverb

What would a book about marriage be without a little financial advice?

These days, it seems, instead of trying to keep up with the Joneses (your neighbors, for those of you too young to recognize this cliché), folks are interested in keeping up with the movie stars or the rich and famous.

> Ada: *"Oh, look, Brad. There's the matching Jean Eric $7,500 purse to go with my Roy Deekulus $3,000 sweater, dear."*
>
> Brad: *"And we could really use another giant screen TV for the bedroom, like the ones we have in the living room and family room and rec room and kitchen. There's a great sale on now."*
>
> Ada: *"Shall we just charge them, or do we need to take some more equity out of the house?"*

The advice that you should live within your income is actually good advice. Pay your credit cards off every month. Save for major purchases and avoid having to pay interest.

It's one thing to argue—I mean have a discussion—about how to spend the money you have. It's quite another to argue about money you don't have. After all, Debt and Depression both start with the letter D. I'm just sayin'.

Bottom line: If you want to keep a smile on your spouse's face, restrain your spending, and match your outgo to your income, minus the 25% you should be saving and the 10% you should be tithing.

⊕

"For which one of you, when he wants to build a tower, does not first sit down and calculate the cost to see if he has enough to complete it?"
—*Luke 14:28*

✠ ◆ ✠

Discussion Questions
1. Think about the arguments or discussions you and your spouse have. What percentage of these disagreements arise from money issues? (Money issues include a sense of inadequate income, spending too much or without consulting the spouse, disagreements over donations to charity, spending money on a relative, and so on.) What are some ways you can resolve these issues before they become arguments?
2. What is a smart, practical, workable way to manage a credit card so that it doesn't become a source of debt and marital disharmony?
3. What makes us so consumption oriented, so hungry to own stuff—stuff that we are likely to throw away sooner rather than later?
4. Do you sometimes feel as if you are programmed to consume?

Small Group Discussion

Research has found that credit cards encourage spending beyond income because there is something almost magical about handing over the plastic (as opposed to handing over cash). Therefore, some counselors advise their clients to establish a budget and then convert the spouses' paychecks into cash. Cash is used to pay for everything, so the couple they never spends more than their income.

1. Does such a plan appeal to you?
2. Is a plan like this practical or too time consuming?
3. Would such a plan work for most people on a tight budget, or would it drive everyone crazy?

Group Activity

Spenders often say they "need" some impulse buy they have just come across. Take a few minutes to discuss the definition of "need." Share several definitions, and discuss which have the most or least merit. Which one will help people restrain their excessive spending?

My Takeaway

Think about what you have learned. What is the most important thing you will take from this chapter? What is your "action item"?

✠
✠ ✠

Prayer

Dear LORD, you have cautioned us through the Apostle Paul, "The love of money is the source of all kinds of evil" (1 Timothy 6:10), and yet we continue to get ourselves into financial and interpersonal difficulties because we keep wanting more and more money to buy more and more stuff.

Help us to realize first, that we were not put here on earth just to consume the products of distant factories and second, that true joy does not come from the abundance of stuff we have packed away in our closets. You created us to love you, not to accumulate future landfill. May we focus our lives on that truth and find there our true happiness. In Jesus' name. Amen.

✝

39
In marriage, expect less and enjoy more.
—Proverb

An unfortunate fact of life these days is that some people marry their own imaginations and neglect to understand the nature of the actual person they married. After the wedding, a crisis occurs, where the spouse does not match—does not live up to—the expectations the other partner had imagined.

When each partner insists that the other change into the expected but imaginary person, more problems arise. (This situation is often referred to as "the big adjustment.")

The truth is that, if you want to be happy, reduce the expectations you have for your spouse and spend some time learning about whom you have actually married.

Another way to express this truth is that the degree of marital satisfaction can be measured by the distance between expectation and reality. The less the distance, the more the satisfaction.

Remember, too, that expectations are self-oriented—what you want—whereas a happy marriage is more likely to result from considering what you can give to the relationship.

Finally, it's one of those mysterious truths that once you eliminate or at least reduce your expectations (which often become demands), and once you start thinking about how you can serve the needs of your spouse, you'll be able to relax and go with the flow. And just when you don't expect it, happiness will ambush you.

✝

Now may the God of hope fill you with all joy and peace in believing, so that you will abound in hope by the power of the Holy Spirit.

—*Romans 15:13*

✠ ♦ ✠

Discussion Questions

1. Before you got married, did you create a list of expectations, "must haves," "must not have," and so on? Now that you have been married for a while, think back and discuss how much or how little your list played in the selection of your spouse. How useful was it? Do the "must haves" correlate well with your spouse's characteristics?
2. How easy or difficult is it to "expect what you get" or "relax and say yes" or "go with the flow" when your spouse "doesn't measure up" to your expectations?
3. Why, do you think, so many couples don't spell out their expectations for the other person before they get married?
4. How easy is it to cross out some of your expectations to make your list shorter and your future spouse more human?

Group Activity
As a group, make a list of typical expectations that newlyweds have for their spouse, for themselves, and for the marriage. For those not married, discuss how reasonable (or not) each expectation appears to be and how likely you think it will be fulfilled. For the married, discuss your experience with some of the expectations and what the eventual outcome was. Include areas of

- Daily tasks (cooking, cleaning, grocery shopping, auto maintenance, yard work, dishwashing, etc.)
- Physical and emotional needs (sympathy, affection and companionship, sex, etc.)
- Practical needs (car, housing, utilities, etc.)

Continue with whatever items have caused friction in the relationships you know about:
1. How were the issues around these unmet expectations resolved?
2. Did the creation and monitoring of lists solve the issue without resentment?

You Be the Counselor
Counsel this couple:

Nan and Dan have been married for a little over a year. They are fond of telling those they meet that they have a solid relationship because they share the most important values. They also say that they are "completely incompatible" because Nan is a "neat freak" who likes to have everything always put away in its proper place, while Dan is a "slob," who leaves the newspaper on the couch, his underwear on the bathroom floor, and dirty dishes in the sink.

> *Dan:* "Ya gotta love her, but Nan thinks that one tiny cookie crumb on the floor is a federal crime."
>
> *Nan:* "I can spend half a day cleaning the house and five minutes after Dan gets home, the place looks as if a tornado has gone through it."
>
> *Dan:* "I can never find my stuff—my reading glasses, my prized fountain pen that my father gave me, my keys, my watch. Sometimes, I can't even find my tablet. Nan always says she has put those things where they belong."
>
> *Nan:* "There is a place for everything."
>
> *Dan:* "I wish she would tell me where those places are."

My Takeaway

Think about what you have learned. What is the most important thing you will take from this chapter? What is your "action item"?

✠
✠ ✠

Prayer

Lord, we don't like being told what to do or where to put things because that seems to offend our sense of autonomy. In other words, we are proud—proud when we tell someone where to put things and proud when we resist. Help us to see you in the order of things, to be neat without being rigidly compulsive. As for being ordered around, we recall that a principal focus of the New Testament is to teach appropriate behavior for Christians.

Lord, help us to remember that you designed the marriage home to be a sanctuary, not an obedience school. You have called us to peace with you and with our spouses. May we fulfill that calling. In Jesus' name. Amen.

Engaged to Be Married (or Just Dating) Activity
Who is expecting what of whom?

For this activity, first write out a list of your top five faults, shortcomings, quirks, habits, and characteristics that you know you have or that others have told you that you have. Rate the prominence of each on a scale of 1 to 10, with 10 being most severe. If you need help in identifying or rating your faults, feel free to ask a friend.

Next, for each of the qualities listed below, evaluate yourself on a scale of 1 to 10, with 10 being best.

Personal Quality	Score
Intelligence	
Moral character and values	
Faith commitment and practice	
Patience	
Emotional strength, Empathy	
Kindness	
Gratitude	
Forgiveness	
Generosity	

With your partner, discuss your list of faults and your Personal Quality ratings and your partner's list and ratings. Explore any differences between how each of you sees the other. Do any of the ratings or discussion change your expectations for marriage?

40

Marriage is a stack of lumber
And a keg of nails;
You have to build it yourself.
If the roof leaks, look to the carpenters.
—Proverb

Yes, the credit for a seamless, watertight marriage goes to God, working through the two carpenters who built it. But credit for the leaky roof goes to the couple alone, who didn't follow the directions very well. (Directions may be found in the Bible.)

If you partner with your spouse, if you put God first in your marriage, and if you agree on the pursuit of common goals, your roof will be less likely to leak.

Remember, when you are building together, you are making a sanctuary, not a coffin.

✠

But the fruit of the Spirit is love, joy, peace, patience, kindness, goodness, faithfulness, gentleness, self-control; against such things there is no law.
–Galatians 5:22-23

✠ ♦ ✠

Additional Commentary

Yes, marriage is a construction project, and even though you might have a first-class set of blueprints, the fact that you and your new spouse are inexperienced almost guarantees that you will have a leaky roof or uneven floors to start with.

But if you continue working together to keep the place fixed up, repairing all the damage that stormy weather and normal wear and tear cause; and if you do not let any "deferred maintenance" cause the place to run down and fall apart, you will enjoy a warm, dry spot to hang your hat, let your hair down, and cuddle.

A key concept here is intentionality. To have a good marriage, you must intend to have a good marriage, paying attention to the needs and wants of your spouse and making all those "repairs" that present themselves, often unexpectedly.

Too many marriages fail simply because one or both spouses were not paying attention to the running down and wearing out of the relationship.

Discussion Questions
1. What does the analogy suggest about marriage when it implies that (every) roof will leak eventually (if not right away) from poor construction techniques or ignorance?
2. What does the analogy imply about the need for constant maintenance and training?
3. What truths about a solid marriage can be deduced from the construction analogy? (Hints: foundation, windy or stormy day, teamwork, helping.)

Group Activity
For a solid book of marital advice, you need a set of blueprints from a reliable architect. Fortunately (as mentioned earlier), many of the nearly

186,000 words of the New Testament consist of instructions for how Christians should behave toward each other.

Have teams of two to four search through the New Testament (focus on Romans 12 through Ephesians 6 to make it easier) and reference ten of the verses that give instructions about how Christians should live with each other, as friends, community members, and as spouses.

Have each team write one or two sentences for each verse, clarifying each, and explaining its importance for marriage and other relationships.

My Takeaway
Think about what you have learned. What is the most important thing you will take from this chapter? What is your "action item"?

✠
✠ ✠
Prayer
Dear LORD, we ask today that you will give us an accurate, mature, open-eyed view of marriage. Prepare us for the difficult journey as we join together as different people facing unknown perils and challenges, yet coming to rely on that solid triangle made from you at the top and each of us at the bottom. And through the success of finding and repairing the leaks in the roof, may we grow more bonded to each other and to you. In Jesus' name we thank you. Amen.

✠

41
Small event, great meaning.
—Proverb

Marriage, like life itself, is about meaning, not experience. In a good marriage, the two spouses build meaning together. Meaning can be built around seemingly small events—a trip to the local coffee house, sharing a pack of gum, eating some tacos on the Tuesday special, reading the Bible together, watching TV and eating popcorn. Or just talking.

When love is active, meaning is everywhere. Don't think you need to fly to a fancy resort halfway across the globe, tightrope walk together across the Grand Canyon, or run down the streets of Pamplona just ahead of 2,000 bulls. You need none of these things to share the deepest meanings. Love adds to the meaning of even the smallest experience. Love creates its own meaning.

So, if you're on a severe budget, don't grind up your soul with regret and envy of the rich. You have each other.

✢

For whoever gives you a cup of water to drink because of your name as followers of Christ, truly I say to you, he will not lose his reward.
—Mark 9:11

✣

It is like a mustard seed, which, when sown upon the soil, though it is smaller than all the seeds that are upon the soil, yet when it is sown, it grows up and becomes larger than all the garden plants and forms large branches; so that the birds of the air can nest under its shade."
—Mark 4:31-32

✠ ◆ ✠

Discussion Questions
1. What "small events" do you remember from your childhood that even today carry great meaning?
2. Describe some things you do with or for your spouse that add meaning to your relationship.
3. Name some of the events you have enjoyed only because your spouse was with you to help create meaning.
4. Why is the meaning of events — and meaning itself — important to the happiness of our lives?
5. Agree or Disagree: "Meaning is created in layers over time. Looking at old photos or other memorabilia, talking about an event again and again at intervals, watching videos, and so on: all these make meaning ever deeper."

Activity for Spouses
For one month, be intentional about saving evidence for all of the outside activities you do with your spouse. Some possibilities include:
- Restaurant receipts
- Movie or sports tickets

- Museum brochure
- Amusement park souvenir
- Piece of a microwave popcorn bag
- Quotation from a book both are reading
- Photo taken at a fun location
- Love notes and cards you sent to each other
- Photo of anything with you and spouse
- Meaningful scriptures
- Photo of a shared devotional page
- A prayer you wrote

1. Make an old-fashioned scrap book, where you paste each item on a separate page. Make a note on each page about the date, time, circumstances, and the meaning that the event holds for you.

OR

2. Post to Facebook photos of the items or photos of you during the activities.

OR

3. Create a YouTube channel and make and post videos of you and your spouse explaining each of the items in "show and tell" style.

OR

4. Create a YouTube (or other social media) channel and write skits starring you and your spouse acting out positive and negative examples of marriage encounters. For example, one skit would demonstrate a hurtful response to an accident, and another would demonstrate a loving, calm response. Making the skits funny might improve their effectiveness.

✠ ♦ ✠

Do a Random Act of Kindness
You don't have to feel nice to be nice.

My Takeaway
Think about what you have learned. What is the most important thing you will take from this chapter? What is your "action item"?

✠
✠ ✠
Prayer

Dear God, you bless us in countless ways, from giving us life and friends and family and our spouses, to material blessings and lifestyle, to the greatest blessing of salvation. We thank you for these wonderful, wonderful things. And may we always remember that it is you, our creator and savior, who has given us our lives, and who continues to give those lives meaning and purpose. In Jesus' name. Amen.

✠

42
In marriage, the journey is the destination.
—Proverb

Marriage, like success, is often misdefined. Some say, wrongly, that success means finally achieving an ultimate goal—of fame, wealth, or power. Actually, success is better defined as making progress toward a worthy goal. Thus, you can be successful over a long period, as long as you are making progress.

Similarly, marriage is often wrongly thought of as "the main chance," the final stage of a relationship, the ultimate goal of perpetual happiness reached at last.

But marriage is not a destination to reach and rest. Nor is it the first step in an ultimate destination (kids? old age? death?). Marriage is a journey you take with your best friend, through many adventures, happy and otherwise. Marriage is a long-term creative problem-solving activity, a trip through many physical and emotional landscapes, a flight of two souls up and down the spiritual ladder from heaven to—well, you get the idea.

Apologies to you realists for my waxing so lyrical, but I wanted to make and rub in the point that marriage is a collection of events, some terminal and some ongoing, some major and most not.

You have probably heard the saying, "Life is what happens while you're making other plans." And since marriage is now a part of your life, its events will happen whether you plan them or not.

Okay, the point is, enjoy the ride. Certainly you want to plan and work toward major milestones. But it's crucial also to explore — and enjoy — your marriage relationship not just in the big goals, like that vacation to Europe, but in the minor events of everyday living:

Sally: "John, the dog barfed on the living room carpet again. Can you bring the pet odor killer?"
John: "Sure, honey. Need anything else?"
Sally: "A couple more rags."
John: "You got 'em."
Sally: "I love you."

You might have heard the saying, "Getting there is half the fun." Double that and you have a marriage. When the ride is smooth, you can embrace sweetly. When you hit the potholes, hold on to each other all the more tightly.

☥

Let love be without hypocrisy. Abhor what is evil; cling to what is good. Be devoted to one another in brotherly love; give preference to one another in honor; not lagging behind in diligence, fervent in spirit, serving the Lord; rejoicing in hope, persevering in tribulation, devoted to prayer. . . .
—*Romans 12:9-12*

Discussion Questions

1. How do the marriage vows ("for better for worse, for richer for poorer, in sickness and in health") connect with this proverb?
2. Here are several definition stems (the beginnings of definitions) that might be used to define marriage. Briefly evaluate each one for use in defining an ideal relationship.

Marriage is
- a process of . . .
- an expectation of . . .
- a solution to . . .
- the development . . .
- the accomplishment of . . .
- the growth of . . .
- the building of . . .
- the cure for . . .
- the search for . . .
- the journey of . . .

4. Which of the following metaphors for marriage seem most applicable for you?
    - Marriage is a quiet gondola ride through the peaceful canals of Venice.
    - Marriage is a ride on a roller coaster with sometimes scary bumps and squeaks.
    - Marriage is a rock climb that requires a partner you can trust.
    - Marriage is a hang glider. If you made it well and fly it together, you'll be safe.

Skit for Commentary

Have the facilitator read the narrator's part and two spouses read the two characters' parts in the story, "The Strange Adventure." Comment on how it relates to this proverb.

THE STRANGE ADVENTURE

Once upon a time, so long ago that it seems like yesterday, circumstances so occurred that two youths found themselves lost together in the desert and forced to spend the night without the services of modern technology.

"What a terrible thing," said the first one. "We're stuck out here all alone among who knows what frightening stuff."

"This is great," said the other. "What an adventure. I can't wait to see what happens."

As the light began to fade, the youths happened upon a snake, sitting on a rock to get the last warmth it could find before the cold night set in.

"Oh, no!" said the first youth. "Out here it's just one problem after another. Now we'll have to worry about that snake crawling all over us as we sleep."

"What a great opportunity," said. the second youth. "Now we can have some dinner." Soon the snake was roasting on an impromptu fire, and in a little while, the two youths began to eat.

"This is horrible," said the first youth, spitting out the meat and nearly vomiting. "I can't imagine a worse thing."

"Actually, it tastes rather mild," said the second youth, eating with relish.

When the next day came and the youths were rescued, they were asked about their adventure.

"It was the most awful, horrible experience I've ever had," said the first youth, trembling from the memory. "I'll be mentally scarred by it for the rest of my life."

"It was great!" said the second youth. "I think it's the best thing that ever happened to me. What a fun time. I'm so glad I was there."

⌘ ***The events we experience are less important than the meaning we give to them, for life is about meaning, not experience.***

✤✤✤

Proverbs for Discussion
1. "Meaning is made, not found."
2. "Marriage is not about what you accomplish together. Marriage is about who you are together."
3. "Every marriage is a journey. And even though sometimes the journey seems to be a horse and buggy ride through the park while other times it seems to be a ride on a burning bus speeding toward a narrow mountain curve, the trip, rightly understood, can shape two souls just the way they need to be shaped."
4. "Shared goals, shared lives, shared love."
5. "Every experience can be seen as an adventure."

My Takeaway
Think about what you have learned. What is the most important thing you will take from this chapter? What is your "action item"?

✠
✠ ✠

PRAYER

Dear LORD, we thank you for always listening to our prayers—which are too often requests and too seldom praises. And we thank you for whatever answers you choose to give us. Remind us, dear God, that as your children, we are called to do great works, but often not easy works. Give us the wisdom to understand how "God gave us a spirit not of fear but of power and love and self-control" (2 Timothy 1:7), that enables us to persevere through every difficult experience, and to find a holy and joyful meaning in it. In Jesus' name. Amen.

✠

43
Marriage math doesn't add up.
—Proverb

Marriage is not a transactional relationship, where spouses exchange one thing or service for another, always making sure they don't get swindled. Marriage is an all-in relationship, where each spouse strives to serve and help the other, without keeping score.

But what does it mean to say that marriage math doesn't add up? Let's look at a couple of examples.

Before they got married, Mike did a certain amount of house cleaning each week. Let's call it 2 housekeeping units (2 HKUs). His soon-to-be bride, Lisa, did three times as much, or 6 HKUs. (That's pretty typical—women are generally much neater than men.)

So, after they get married, both Mike and Lisa are thinking they will be sharing housekeeping tasks (Mike is such a good guy), and they both think this means having to do only half as much work as before, with their loving spouse doing the other half.

Okay, so they get married. Now, let's do the math. Mike reduces his work to 1 HKU per week. Lisa reduces her work to 3 HKUs per week. Mike thinks everything is fine, as both have reduced their housekeeping by half. But to Lisa, Mike is doing only one third of what she expected him to do. She thinks that when she reduced her work by 3 HKUs, Mike would do the other 3. Tension results. Maybe even conflict.

In the example above, Lisa probably thinks Mike should conform to her model of housekeeping. But that would mean that, while she enjoys cutting her housekeeping work by half, Mike would have to increase his work by half. Marriage math just doesn't add up.

Here's another example of marriage math gone wrong:

> Sandy: *I realize that marriage is a give-and-take relationship. So, when I get married, I expect to give fifty percent and get fifty percent.*

Sandy is in for a rude awakening, because she is a scorekeeper—someone who plans to keep track of who does what, and to make sure that everything in the marriage is "fair." But scorekeepers, without realizing their bias toward themselves, tend to add 25 points to their side while subtracting 25 points from their spouse's side.

In fact, marriage math is so wacky that, for Sandy's determination to give 50 percent and take 50 percent, while her spouse will do the same, she will find that 50 plus 50 equals 25. And that's why, even if both spouses pledge to make a 100 percent effort, the scorekeeper isn't going to be happy.

Advice: Don't keep score. The numbers just don't add up. Instead, give and serve, give and serve. Or as it's sometimes put, "See a job, do a job."

☦

Do all things without grumbling or disputing; so that you will prove yourselves to be blameless and innocent, children of God above reproach in the midst of a crooked and perverse generation, among whom you appear as lights in the world....
   —Philippians 2:14-15

✠ ♦ ✠

Discussion Questions
1. How effective do you think a scorekeeping system can work in a marriage? Explain why you think as you do.
2. Do you know any marriages where one spouse is a scorekeeper and the other isn't? What is the result?
3. Do you know any marriages where both spouses are scorekeepers? Does their system work well?
4. Can you think of alternative systems for sharing the tasks of marriage? Think of fairer, easier, less measurement of the other person's effort, yet still effective.

Group Activity
Together in pairs or small groups, devise a scorekeeping system that lists common tasks and assigns a score to each task. Examples might include:
- Cook dinner (x points)
- Vacuum living room (x points)

- Take out trash (x points)

Identify areas where you find difficulty, such as

- How precisely can the scope of a task be defined?
- How is agreement reached on whether a task has been done and how well it must be done (who does the measuring)?
- How is agreement reached on how many points are assigned to each task?

What are your conclusions about scorekeeping? Can it be made easy, practical, consistent, and provide a harmonious relationship?

My Takeaway

Think about what you have learned. What is the most important thing you will take from this chapter? What is your "action item"?

✠
✠ ✠

Prayer

Thank you, LORD, for designing marriage as a partnership, giving us the opportunity to share and divide the tasks of living together. Grant us wisdom and agreement in how we handle the labors of life so that we can clean through the grime of reality together with cheerful and loving hearts. In Jesus' name we pray. Amen.

✞

44
Once forgiven, twice forgotten.
—Proverb

This proverb serves to remind us that once we forgive a spouse for some wrongdoing, that wrongdoing must never be mentioned again, especially in the context of a dispute.

During an argument, some spouses have a tendency to bring up every past wrong they can remember, as a form of additional ammunition.

However, bringing up a past wrong has no relevance to the current situation. Its only purpose is to inflict emotional harm on the spouse.

Moreover, to remember a transgression from the past and to bring it up again during an argument means that it was never really forgiven before. Instead, it has been harbored and nurtured and held as a grudge, waiting to be flung in the face of the wrongdoer during the next disagreement.

> **You can't change the past, so why bring it up?**

If you sincerely forgive a wrong, put it from your mind; forget it. Then, if during an argument, the wrong comes to mind again, forget it again. Do not mention it. It's a dead issue.

"For if you forgive others for their transgressions, your heavenly Father will also forgive you. But if you do not forgive others, then your Father will not forgive your transgressions."
—Matthew 6:14-15

Discussion Questions
1. "Forgive and forget—like that's going to happen!" expresses a common view of the proverb. Why is letting go of a wrong done to us so difficult? Is there a solution to this?
2. Don't some people during an argument actually exult in the power to hurt the other that remembering the wrong gives them? What is the source of that, and how can it be profitably addressed?
3. Does the severity of the wrong affect the length of time needed to forgive it? Explain.
4. Have you ever tried to forgive someone who wronged you deeply, but you found it impossible to do so right away? How did the situation ultimately turn out?
5. Do you find it difficult to forgive? Explain the process you use, and say how effective it is.

> **Forgiveness**
> **Is the Blessing of Renewed Life**
> The ability, willingness, and desire to forgive each other is a fundamental requirement for a happy marriage.

Group Activity
In small groups, discuss the problem of forgiveness of wrongs, with emphasis on these items:
1. How quickly should or can someone be forgiven?
2. Which methods work best and which least?
3. Does a wrongdoer need to repent and ask for forgiveness before he or she can be forgiven?
4. How can bringing up forgiven wrongs be prevented in future arguments?

You Be the Counselor
Counsel this couple:

> Wayne: "Did you scratch my car again?"
>
> Jayne: "I don't know what you're talking about."
>
> Wayne: "That's a lie. Just like the lie when you lied to me in 2015 about being late for lunch, supposedly because of car trouble — car trouble named Jack, if I recall."
>
> Jayne: "Well, you started flirting with that sexy home wrecking floozy in the summer of 2000. You said she was an intern. Hah!"
>
> Wayne: "That was another one of your jealousy delusions, like that time in 1986 when you ruined Christmas by intentionally pouring paint all over my car because I barely looked at some waitress. And then you repeatedly denied it. Talk about a liar, liar."
>
> Jayne: "Barely looked?! I could have filled a five-gallon bucket with your drool."
>
> Wayne: "Maybe I glanced at her once or twice, but I didn't throw myself at her like you did with that Tom guy in 1982, or Bill at the football game in 1973. I'll bet you don't even remember what the score was."
>
> Jayne. "I didn't throw myself at them, as you say. You and I weren't married then, so it's none of your business, anyway."
>
> Wayne: "Liar."

Activity

1. Locate a thesaurus and look up all the synonyms for *forgive, forgiveness, forgiving, forgiven.*
2. Get a good dictionary (either unabridged or a collegiate) and write out in detail the meaning of five of the words you found. Discuss.
3. Have you gained any new insight into the concept? Explain.

Biblical Imperative

The Lord's Prayer was given to the disciples by Jesus as a model for praying and living. What does it say about forgiveness? What does Jesus say will happen to those who don't forgive others? (See Matthew 6:9-15)

My Takeaway

Think about what you have learned. What is the most important thing you will take from this chapter? What is your "action item"?

✠
✠ ✠

Prayer

Our dear LORD God, why is forgiveness so hard? Your son Jesus forgave the Jewish authorities and the Roman executioners even while he was being tortured by crucifixion on a cross. And yet we sometimes bear grudges for years over the slightest offense. Melt our hearts with pity and sympathy, dear God, for those who foolishly, selfishly, or especially inadvertently wrong us. You have commanded us to forgive; help us to obey. In Jesus' name. Amen.

✠

45
If married love and joy come to an end,
To blame your mate is spitting in the wind.
—Proverb

Let's just assume that, if there is sand in the machinery of your marriage, you were both at the beach earlier; so it's better to work together to clean out the grit than to try to figure out just whose sand it is.

I know, I know, it's not you. It's all your partner's problem. But here's a thought: If your marriage is troubled, *pray that it's all your fault*.

Huh? Well, look at it this way. The only person you can change is you. So, if the unhappiness and frustration in the marriage are on your side, there's hope! You can change! Your marriage can get better!

Remember, you can't change your spouse—except by modeling the Golden Proverb[11] to such an extent that your spouse will choose to change out of love and gratitude.

✢

"Why do you look at the speck that is in your brother's eye, but do not notice the log that is in your own eye? Or how can you say to your brother, 'Let me take the speck out of your eye,' and behold, the log is in your own eye?

---

[11] On page 188.

You hypocrite, first take the log out of your own eye, and then you will see clearly to take the speck out of your brother's eye."
—*Matthew 7:3-5*

✠ ◆ ✠

Discussion Questions

1. How fast can you name your spouse's top three major flaws?
2. How fast can you name your own top three major flaws?
3. How fast can your spouse name your top three major flaws?
4. How fast can your spouse name his or her own top three flaws?
5. Someone has said that as their marriage ages, some spouses become much more picky and intolerant of the other spouse's shortcomings, while other spouses become much less picky and more tolerant of their spouse's "idiosyncrasies." Which marriages do you think are happier and why? (For example, are the "more tolerant" marriages really only a union of quiet, teeth-grinding resentment?)

The Krazy Kounselor Speaks

Several young people approached the Krazy Kounselor and said, "We are terrified of choosing the wrong person to marry. What if we marry a slob or a neat freak or someone with even more intolerable flaws?"

The Krazy Kounselor replied, "When you are dating, keep both eyes open."

"What about after we are married?" the young people asked.

"After you are married," said the Krazy Kounselor, "keep one eye closed and the other eye shut."

"That's crazy," the young people said.

Overheard for Discussion

1. "In each relational dispute, there is not only enough blame for each partner to have a full plate, but enough left over to choke a horse."
2. "Many people mistakenly believe that the purpose of an argument is to prove the other person wrong—and possibly to damage them emotionally. Actually, the purpose of an argument should be to find truth, act on it, and restore the relationship."
3. "Criticizing, complaining, nagging, and whining to your spouse that everything is your spouse's fault will soon deliver you from all those problems—because your spouse will leave."
4. "It takes two to Tango."

My Takeaway

Think about what you have learned. What is the most important thing you will take from this chapter? What is your "action item"?

✠
✠ ✠

Prayer

Dear LORD, we all know the feeling of being criticized, blamed, and faulted by our spouse. And we have been guilty of criticizing and blaming in return. Help us to become mature and fair in our disagreements, always seeking truth and peace, and showing love and respect. We thank you in Jesus' name. Amen.

✠

46

Be to your spouse
What you want your spouse
To be to you.
— The Golden Proverb

Say this out loud: "If I am critical, disrespectful, controlling, negative, cold, rejecting, and resentful toward my spouse, my spouse will become warm, affectionate, loving, kind, and happy." How does that sound? Not very plausible? So then, why do some spouses behave as if they believe this?

Now say this out loud: "If I am warm, affectionate, loving, kind, and happy with my spouse, my spouse will be the same with me." Does that seem to be at least a little more likely?

The original Golden Rule, of course, was meant to be a rule of personal moral behavior, not a method for creating reciprocal behavior. But in marriage, the Golden Proverb does, in fact, work. And it works both ways: Spouses tend to treat each other the way they are treated.

✟

Finally, brethren, whatever is true, whatever is honorable, whatever is right, whatever is pure, whatever is lovely, whatever is of good repute, if there is any excellence and if anything worthy of praise, dwell on these things.
—Philippians 4:8

Discussion Questions

1. Implied in the Golden Proverb, "Be to your spouse what you want your spouse to be to you," is the truth that, as different as men and women are from each other, both sexes share a need for emotional approval and acceptance. What are some other psychological and emotional characteristics that men and women share, as relates to living with each other?
2. If acting the way we would like our spouse to act is our goal, why do we so often fail to model those behaviors?
3. When we see the same failings in our spouse as we see in ourselves, why do we judge our spouses by a harsher standard than the one we apply to ourselves?

> **Know Yourself**
> Ask, "Am I the kind of person someone would look forward to coming home to each day?"

My Takeaway

Think about what you have learned. What is the most important thing you will take from this chapter? What is your "action item"?

PRAYER

Dear LORD, let us begin today on the path to a happier marriage for ourselves and for our spouses by truly adopting the Golden Proverb as our guide to behavior in our marriage. In Jesus' name. Amen.

47
Maturity can be measured
By the size of what upsets you.
— Proverb

Some people become furious when there is a small piece of gristle in the steak, when the toilet paper roll isn't replaced, or when a dish is left in the sink instead of being put in the dishwasher. If one spouse paid fifty cents more for the same item that was on sale for less elsewhere, the other spouse thinks a hateful, demeaning attack is justified.

And then there are those spouses who ignore, tolerate, or forgive not only small irregularities like those described above, but also substantial mistakes. Call this maturity, or love, or understanding — or perspective.

Speaking of perspective, here is a little story that might help you understand that in the overall context of life and marriage, little differences from what you prefer are really not so important after all.

UNEXPECTED NEWS

Mrs. Jones walked sternly into the living room and glared at Mr. Jones. "You left the cap off the toothpaste tube again," she said harshly. "Why can't you ever remember to put it back on? It's not that hard. Even a child can do it."

"And why can't you ever remember to turn off the coffee pot?" retorted Mr. Jones. "It was still on

when I got home this evening. I swear, one day you're going to burn the house down."

"Maybe I'd remember to turn off the coffee pot if I wasn't so distracted by having to pick up your dirty socks and underwear, which you leave all over the house. You know, there is a hamper to put your dirty clothes in, right next to that big white box called a washing machine. Do you want me to show you where it is?"

"Speaking of washing, I noticed the other day that you use way too much shampoo. And you buy that expensive salon junk which isn't any better than the cheap brand."

Just as Mrs. Jones was about to deliver a snarling response to Mr. Jones, as they both were gearing up for another heated, three-hour argument, the phone rang. Mr. Jones moved his glare from his wife to the phone as he answered it: "Yeah, what is it?"

"Hello. This is Officer Clayton Smith. Is Mr. John Jones available"?

"This is John Jones. What do you want?" Mr. Jones demanded.

"Mr. Jones, do you have a daughter named Jennifer Nicole Jones?"

"Yes, yes," answered Mr. Jones, testily. "What has she done this time?"

"I'm sorry," said Officer Smith, "but your daughter was in an automobile accident this evening. The driver lost control and crashed. Your daughter was trapped inside when the car exploded in flames."

✞

So, as those who have been chosen of God, holy and beloved, put on a heart of compassion, kindness, humility, gentleness and patience; bearing with one another, and forgiving each other, whoever has a complaint against anyone; just as the Lord forgave you, so also should you. Beyond all these things put on love, which is the perfect bond of unity. Let the peace of Christ rule in your hearts, to which indeed you were called in one body; and be thankful.
—*Colossians 3:12-15*

✠ ♦ ✠

Discussion Questions
1. Why do some people get so upset over such seemingly minor issues as those mentioned in the opening discussion and the Joneses' argument?
2. If the proverb for this entry is correct, how "mature" would you judge yourself? In other words, what upsets you and why?
3. Why are we sometimes resistant to getting upset, even over relatively large errors, but other times a minor issue "pushes our buttons" and we explode in anger?
4. Analyze and discuss the method of argument Mr. and Mrs. Jones use. Here are some hints to get you started.
    - *glared at Mr. Jones*
    - *said harshly*
    - *why can't you ever remember (says Mrs. Jones)*
    - *even a child can do it*
    - *why can't you ever remember (says Mr. Jones)*

Group Discussion
The value of seeing things in context — the context of life outside our own experience — is that we gain a much larger perspective on life and the events that shape our world. What events have you learned about through reading, watching the news, or listening to others that have broadened your perspective on life and have made some things that earlier seemed very important now seem not so important?

More Perspectives
Perspective is a great clarifier of values. Discuss what and how each of these vignettes helps us gain perspective about some aspect of life. How do these vignettes affect our values?

1. *"I used to complain that I couldn't afford the new fancy shoes I wanted, until I met a man who had no feet."*

2. *Julie: "Oh, Sarah, this is the worst day of my life. I've got a huge zit on my nose and the prom is tonight. Are you coming?"*
   Sarah: "I'm so sorry, Julie. I can't make it. I've just been diagnosed with pancreatic cancer and I need to start chemotherapy today."

3. *Officer Doright: "These old junk cars are an offense to the eyes and a violation of trash dumping laws, Mr. Handy. You're facing a $10,000 fine."*
   Mr. Handy: "Give me a wrench and three days." Three days later seven needy townspeople were driving around in free cars.

My Takeaway
Think about what you have learned. What is the most important thing you will take from this chapter? What is your "action item"?

✠
✠ ✠
PRAYER

Dear LORD, it seems that sometimes we spend a lot of wasted time, effort, grief, blame, fault-finding, and hostility trying to identify the crime, the guilty, and the required punishment for every minor infraction of our personal Book of Crimes. Then we have to deliver the punishment with the right critical words, the right hostile tone of voice and the right rejecting body language. And all this just to hurt someone we love because our ego has been bruised.

Help us, O LORD, to revise our own hearts so that we will not need to suppress the urge to be hurtful, and not need to forgive the minor faults we see every day, because we don't even feel the urge or see the faults to begin with. In Jesus' name we thank you deeply. Amen.

✞

48

Your husband is not your father
That you should punish him,
Nor your brother that you should rival him.
Your wife is not your mother
That you should take her for granted,
Nor your sister
That you should compete with her.
— Proverb

This proverb is a reminder to check your emotional baggage to see if you have unresolved issues with a parent or sibling that you might unknowingly transfer onto your spouse.

This transfer seems to occur with some frequency, so it needed to be mentioned. It's unjust to get revenge on your father by punishing your husband or to even the score with your sister by treating your wife as a competitor or an enemy.

✞

"For this reason a man shall leave his father and mother, and the two shall become one flesh; so they are no longer two, but one flesh."
—*Mark 10:7-8*

✠ ◆ ✠

Discussion Questions

1. Do you see any similarities in the faults you see in your spouse and those you see in your parents or siblings?
2. Think about what emotion accompanies your urge to correct your spouse's faults. Do you feel love, compassion, anger, hostility, revenge?
3. Discuss the song lyric, "I want a girl just like the girl that married dear old dad."
4. Before you were married, were you conscious of wanting to marry someone just like (or completely unlike) your mother or father?
5. Is it easier to change your behavior toward your spouse if you recognize that it reflects your behavior toward a relative?

Activity

(Note: This activity might require a substantial amount of time. If your book study group meets regularly, you might want to use a set amount of time each meeting to catch up on progress and discuss.)

1. Organize into groups of 5 to 7. Discuss the question, "What faults are the most commonly perceived in spouses (divided by men and women)?"
2. Compare each demographic in your group's lists with those of the other group.
3. How much agreement or variance do you find? Is there any general agreement?
4. Now compare each demographic (men, mothers, etc.) and determine how similar or different they are.
5. Discuss your overall conclusions. Did the children inherit the faults of their parents?
6. Is identifying and tracking faults really worth the time and effort?

> **Do a Random Act of Kindness**
> Write down and share with your spouse each day one good thing they said or did.

My Takeaway

Think about what you have learned. What is the most important thing you will take from this chapter? What is your "action item"?

☩
☩ ☩

PRAYER

Dear LORD, your Scriptures are filled with statements about the value and use of knowledge and understanding. Help us to gain the knowledge and understanding we need in order to develop a true and encompassing perspective, seeing ourselves, our spouses and the entire world in the context of your love and your will. We thank you and bless you for all that you do and for all that you are. In Jesus' name. Amen.

☩

49
To find your marriage, lose yourself.
— Proverb

Even casual observation of happily married couples reveals that the key to a warm and loving relationship is that both spouses have learned to get themselves — their egos — off the throne of their hearts, put Jesus on the throne, and become humble servants of each other. By contrast, unhappily married couples have super-glued themselves to their own thrones.

The problem is pride. Pride equals me, self, selfish, my way, my standards, my needs, my decisions, my power, my control. Pride is judgmental, critical, demanding, scorekeeping, contentious.

Humility is a focus on others. It is selfless, accepting, grateful, serving, giving, thoughtful, deferential.

It's just a bit of a challenge to get close to or feel loving toward a dictator who acts as if you just don't measure up. A good marriage features the embrace of souls, a comfortable, warm-hearted twining of affection. In order to have this, you and your spouse must both yield — you must lose yourself — and team up to work as one.

Instead of thinking about "me, my, and mine," think about what you can do to fulfill your spouse's needs and wants, how you can give of yourself instead of taking for yourself, what you can do for the team. You'll get a lot more satisfaction—and even happiness—than you will from a prideful obsession with yourself.

☦

And all of you, clothe yourselves with humility toward one another, for God is opposed to the proud, but gives grace to the humble.
—1 Peter 5:5

☩ ◆ ☩

Discussion Questions
1. Have you ever met or observed someone who was too proud to be happy? Describe the situation.
2. It is sometimes said that "pride is its own punishment." Comment.
3. Some have claimed that Pride, the foremost of the traditional Seven Deadly Sins, is really the father of the other six sins. Explain how being proud can foster Anger, Greed, Lust, Sloth, Gluttony, and Envy.

A Story
Read the following vignette and explain how the man's pride damaged his desire for learning.

ONLY THE HUMBLE CAN LEARN
A man approached Diogenes and begged to become the great philosopher's disciple. Diogenes gave him a fish to carry and told the man to follow him. The man, out of shame, threw the fish away and left.

A few days later, Diogenes saw the man in the marketplace and told him, "Your commitment to our rela-

tionship and to your learning was so weak that it was destroyed by a dead fish." — *from Diogenes Laertius*

Another Story

Read and discuss the point of the following story. Does it present a truth about people (the plumber, the doctor)?

After reading the story, explain what is meant by the saying, "The cost to repair the toilet is determined by the kind of car parked in the driveway of the house."

Pride Is Its Own Punishment

Once there was a man named Paul Pence, MD. He was very proud of being a medical doctor, so he mentioned that fact at every opportunity.

It happened one day that Dr. Pence needed his plumbing repaired. He told Mrs. Pence to call the plumber, because Dr. Pence was "too busy."

Soon, the plumber came out to the house and looked at the problem. "What ya got here, Lady," the plumber said, after he made his analysis, "is what ya call a mainline backup. I can fix it for $150."

Mrs. Pence told the plumber that she would have to get her husband's approval, since she had no idea either what a mainline back up was or how much it should cost to clear up the problem.

Soon Dr. Pence arrived. "Well," he said. "So you are the plumber. I am Dr. Pence, MD. I assume that even with only a high school education a common tradesman like you has had sufficient experience to discover a common cause of the problem. What is your assessment of the cost?"

"He told me $150," said Mrs. Pence.

"Well," said the plumber, noticing that Dr. Pence was rocking gently back and forth with satisfaction over his supposedly exalted social status, "you didn't give me a chance to finish. The $150 covers just the excavation.

Then there is the cleanout, the new pipe, any permits, the fill in – "

"Come, come, little man," said Dr. Pence, testily, "I have an important phone call coming up. Just tell me what the total is."

"All told, Dr. Pence," said the plumber, "the whole job is going to set you back $7,450."

"That seems high," said Dr. Pence, who knew nothing about plumbing.

"Did I tell you that your Exito Superflush XL Draineate seals need to be repaired? The chrome plating alone on those is $900."

"Well, okay," said Dr. Pence.

You Be the Counselor
Counselor: "So how is your marriage going?"
Biff: "Not very well."
Counselor: "What is the area of your discontent? Communication, togetherness, recreation, sex, cooking, emotional connection, finances, fun, problem solving, spending too much?"
Biff: "Yes, all of the above. I thought I'd get much more out of marriage than I'm getting."
Counselor: "What are you putting into your marriage to make it work?"
Biff: "Huh?! What are you talking about?"

If useful, quote and discuss these proverbs with Biff:

- "People who marry only for what they can get rather than what they can give are first labeled *foolish*, and later, *divorced*."
  —Anonymous
- "You rescue the humble, but you look for ways to put down the proud."
  —2 Samuel 22:28 (CEV)
- "All who belong to the LORD, show how you love him. The LORD protects the faith-

ful, but he severely punishes everyone who is proud." —Psalm 31:23 (CEV)
- "Evil people are proud and arrogant, but sin is the only crop they produce."
 —Proverbs 21:4 (CEV)

My Takeaway
Think about what you have learned. What is the most important thing you will take from this chapter? What is your "action item"?

✠
✠ ✠

PRAYER

LORD, we know from your word in the Bible that pride is our enemy and that humility is the attitude that pleases you. But we also know that a fundamental flaw in our human nature is the often unsuppressed egotism that keeps us from loving others and deferring to them and serving them.

In marriage we sometimes let our pride and selfishness get the better of us and we struggle for conquest, victory, control, rule, domination—anything other than a truth that might not be in our favor.

Dear God, give us the wisdom, the sense of justice and fairness, and the kindness that we need to keep our silly egos out of our spousal relationships and work with, not against, our companion and coworker for the kingdom. In Jesus' name we thank you. Amen.

✠

50
Criticizing your spouse for an accident
Pours salt into an open wound.
—Proverb

Suppose your spouse drops grandma's favorite gravy bowl, or knocks over the iced tea glass in a restaurant when you are out to dinner together. What is your reaction? Do you get angry and say something like, "Why can't you be more careful?" or "That was grandma's pride and joy and now it's ruined forever. What's wrong with you? Must you be so clumsy?"

Let's think about this. The definition of an accident is an unfortunate event occurring without intent. The person responsible didn't want it to happen and feels unhappy that it did happen and needs comfort and reassurance that the misadventure is survivable.

Therefore, responding with angry criticism not only deprives your spouse of the support and compassion he or she needs, but it compounds the feelings of guilt, sorrow, and regret without adding a grain of sand toward repairing the loss. Worse, it telegraphs to your spouse that you cannot be relied on to offer aid and comfort in times of emotional distress: You won't be the go-to person when your spouse is facing the stressors and failures we all encounter in our ordinary experience.

Here's a story drawn from real life.

I opened the cupboard where the spices are kept and a glass pepper grinder fell out onto the floor and shattered, throwing glass and peppercorns all over the kitchen. When my wife got home, we had a choice of three ways to interact about this event.

(1) My wife could blame the accident on me. *"Oh, that was my only pepper grinder, and my only whole peppercorns. How could you have been so careless? You just don't care about my things, do you? And now I'll have to wear shoes in the kitchen to avoid stepping on broken glass, because the way you clean up, there will still be shards all over the place. And the poor dog will probably cut his feet and then get blood all over the carpet. I hope you're happy."*

(2) I could blame the accident on my wife. *"When I opened the cupboard, the pepper grinder fell out and shattered all over the place. Now I have to clean it up. You must have carelessly put it in an unsafe position. I could have been cut by the glass when it fell out. Why can't you be more careful when you put things away?"*

(3) What really happened.
Me: *"We've had an accident. When I opened the cupboard, the pepper grinder fell out on the floor and broke. I need to clean it up before we can eat dinner."*
My wife: *"How can I help you clean it up?"*
Me: *"Where's a broom?"*
My wife: *"I'll get it. What else do you need?"*
Me: *"Maybe the vacuum."*

My wife: "I'll sweep it up."
Me: "No, I'll do it. You relax."

Quiz Time:
1. Which of the three scenarios would you have chosen, and what would the resulting interaction have been like?
2. How would your chosen scenario have impacted your long-term relationship with your spouse?
3. Would that impact be worth it?

✠

So then we pursue the things which make for peace and the building up of one another.
—Romans 14:19

By accident—or by appointment—just as I was preparing this book's expanded edition, the same point was reinforced. My wife and I were in the kitchen putting dishes away. I remarked that our inventory of glasses was diminishing. She said that sometimes one gets broken. Just at that moment, I heard a loud crash and saw glass fragments scattering across the floor.

We were both so amazed at the coincidence that we just had to stand there a moment, laughing. Then we swept, vacuumed, and wiped up the pieces.

✠ ♦ ✠

Discussion Questions
1. Why do so many people feel the urge to criticize or at least make a negative or critical comment when another person has an accident?
2. In what sense is criticizing someone for an accident "blaming the victim"?
3. Read the "story drawn from real life" again. Why do some people rush to blame someone else when an accident occurs?
4. What are some possible supportive phrases or sentences you might use when a spouse or friend has an accident?
5. Discuss the meaning of the Accident Poster below.

Accident	
1a unpredicted, **unintended** event **b** occurring **without planning or intention:** by chance **2a** an unfortunate event resulting from **unwanted** circumstances **3a** an unexpected event causing loss or damage **but not the fault of the one experiencing the loss or damage b** undesigned, unanticipated, **unwanted** negative event	misfortune mishap misadventure fluke affliction fortuity tragedy bad luck chance event randomness

Dialogue Discussion
Discuss this interaction between Jonni and Lorry.

Jonni: "Oops! I dropped the casserole!"

Lorry: "What?? Aaaah!! It smashed all over the floor! What have you done? The dinner is ruined!! What am I going to do? How could you – ."

Jonni: "I'm so sorry. It was an accident."

> *Lorry: "You should have been more careful. Now we'll have to serve our guests grocery store frozen lasagna. That will sure make a great impression."*
>
> *Jonni: "I didn't mean for the pan to slip out of my hands. It just did."*
>
> *Lorry: "Well, I forgive you – this time. Just be more careful from now on."*

My Takeaway

Think about what you have learned. What is the most important thing you will take from this chapter? What is your "action item"?

✠
✠ ✠

Prayer

Dear LORD, all of us have accidents with distressing regularity, and sometimes we are hard on ourselves over them, even though we are fully aware that we had no intention of causing the problem. But even if we do blame ourselves, we soon let our sorrow give way to acceptance. And we do the best we can to minimize the damage.

May we, dear God, with your help, be a comfort and reassurance to those who unintentionally cause an accident. And may we apply double kindness and sympathy and reassurance to our spouses when they are the cause.

May we never use an innocent accident as an excuse to insult our precious life partner. In Jesus' name we pray. Amen.

✠

51
Anger brings loss.
[Hasira, hasara.]
—Swahili proverb

Remember this two-word Swahili proverb (which literally means "anger, loss" or "anger, damage") next time you are tempted to lash out at your spouse, who is or ought to be your best friend and the love of your life.

Enough said.

☦

Do not let the sun go down on your anger.
—*Ephesians 4:26b*

Discussion Questions
1. How many of the following proverbs do you recognize?
    - The kind man loses his shirt, but the angry man gets rich quickly.
    - Those who stomp around wrathfully are loved by all.
    - Answer a calm objection with an irate stream of curses and everyone will call you wise.

   If you don't recognize any of these proverbs, perhaps it is because they are not actual proverbs. But why not? Explain what is wrong about them.

2. Just what does it mean to say that anger brings or causes loss? What kind of loss?
3. When you recover from being angry with someone, how do you feel? If it varies, what is the source of the variation?
4. All things considered, is anger a good tool to keep in your marital tool box? Explain.

My Takeaway

Think about what you have learned. What is the most important thing you will take from this chapter? What is your "action item"?

✠
✠ ✠

Prayer

Lord, we know that often a thoughtful disagreement is justified, and occasionally our annoyance is understandable, but we also know that many times we overreact and allow our pride to take over our thoughts and blow a minor issue out of context and proportion. Such a selfish focus on ourselves and the determination to win at all costs can result only in turning what could have been a successful problem solving session into an "all participants lose" battle.

Please help us to remember that anger is not the friend of truth, not the friend of accuracy, not the friend of problem solving, and not the friend of loving relationships. We thank you, in Jesus' name. Amen.

✠

52
A cheerful wife is the spice of life.
—French proverb

As has been said by many observers, men are simple creatures when it comes to relationships with women. Men want their wives to offer them respect, affirmation, and encouragement. A husband interprets a cheerful, happy wife as embodying all these things, making him feel as if he is doing well. And he is motivated to do things to keep her happy.

If his wife is not cheerful, if there always seems to be something wrong—especially if it's something wrong with him—the husband feels that he doesn't measure up and becomes discouraged. Unhappiness, drama, and discontent in a wife put enormous stress on husbands, who often try not to show it. But the proverb is true—no, it's understated: A cheerful wife is her husband's delight.

Happy Wife, Happy Life

✠

Is anyone cheerful? He is to sing praises.
—James 5:13b

✠ ♦ ✠

Discussion Questions

1. It has been noted by many marriage therapists that wives most often control the emotional climate of a marriage. Hence the saying, "Happy wife, happy life." It has also been noted that when one spouse smiles at the other, the smile (and happy feeling) is contagious and often causes the other spouse to smile and be happy, too. Have you had this experience in your own marriage or seen the same reaction in the relationships of others?
2. A number of men were asked, "What is one thing that makes your wife happy?" Many of the men answered, "Nothing."
3. When men were asked, "What is the most important thing you would like to see in your wife? Most answered, "That she would be happy or content." Why, do you think, there are so many unhappy wives? Some answers that have been given:
    - Wives feel powerless and controlled by husbands who dominate them.
    - Wives have too many expectations on them, and they still feel obligated to perform to the best standards.
    - Wives are over stressed and over tired from the constant addition of new roles: Job and career, husband, housekeeper ("chief cook and bottle washer" they used to joke), child raiser, and now for many, elder care for aging parents.

Happiness might be a difficult character attribute to measure, but see if you can interview several people, both male and female, and ask them where they would place themselves on a "Cheerfulness Scale." (Idea: 10 is "always cheerful or happy," and 1 is "never cheerful or happy.")

Report your results to your group.
- Are the women you surveyed less happy than the men? If so, why?

4. When a young woman in her twenties is asked, "Why are you in love with that guy?" a common answer is, "He makes me happy." When a woman over 30 is asked the same question, the answer is usually different. Discuss.

Scripture

"When a man takes a new wife, he shall not go out with the army nor be charged with any duty; he shall be free at home one year and shall give happiness to his wife whom he has taken."
—Deuteronomy 24:5

My Takeaway

Think about what you have learned. What is the most important thing you will take from this chapter? What is your "action item"?

✠
✠ ✠

PRAYER

LORD, we know that our spouses are not responsible for our happiness, but that each of us alone has the obligation to seek the path of service that leads first to contentment, then to happiness, and then to joy.

Help us never to blame anyone else for any lack of happiness we may feel. Help us instead to pursue the path of righteousness, always showing a cheerful demeanor, and a dedication to living in the joy of the LORD. With gratitude we ask in Jesus' name. Amen.

✠

53
Marriage is a dance.
—Proverb

This concluding proverb reminds us of the key truths about marriage. This is truly marriage in a nutshell:

1. Someone has to lead. In a Biblical, Christian marriage, this is the husband. (Thinking that "When we disagree, we'll just compromise," doesn't always work.) Let your husband lead and you might be surprised how often he defers to his wife.
2. The two partners must learn to move together as one unit. Unless you dance as one, your movement will be called "stepping on feet," or "falling down" rather than "dancing."
3. Practice over time improves your skill. As a friend once said about her own marriage, "It gets better." It gets better if you are intentional about it and unselfish in your aims.
4. The most beautiful dances require that you keep each other close and hold on.
5. The meaning of the dance is something beyond either partner individually. (It's about the dance, not about you.)
6. The more the combined and focused energy, the more amazing the dance.
7. Two people dancing together is a lot more fun than one person trying to dance alone.

Marriage is to be held in honor among all....
—Hebrews 13:4a

Discussion Questions
1. Newly married couples often face conflict because they are still trying to "do their own dance," rather than dancing together as one. Discuss how learning to dance together translates into learning to live together. Some ideas to explore might be:
   - Trust each other
   - Relax and don't be afraid
   - Learn about each other's expectations
   - Talk and clarify, talk and clarify
   - Put your assumptions on the table
2. Some people object to the idea of the husband as the leader of the marriage relationship. Discuss what it means to be a leader and how leadership is or should be exercised in a marriage.
3. Instead of the metaphor, "Marriage is a dance," what other image can you think of that helps clarify the attributes of the relationship?

You Be the Counselor
Jan and Jim have been getting along mostly very well, and are planning to marry in the next year or so. However, they have discovered a conflict in their personalities that is threatening the relationship. How would you counsel them?

Jim: "I work for a local television station, and we have to have everything ready to go well in advance of air time. The 6 O'clock News has to start at 6:00, not 6:15 or even 6:01. I am

> used to organizing the rest of my life the same way. Jan, on the other hand, doesn't take deadlines or appointments seriously. She's always barely on time or even a few minutes late. Her excuse is that clocks differ, and I must have looked at a faster clock than she did. It's driving me crazy."
>
> Jen: "Jim needs to lighten up and relax. I don't see the point of arriving twenty or thirty minutes early just to sit in the seats watching the ads before the movie begins."
>
> Jim: "I hate arriving at the theater after the movie has been going on for ten minutes. It spoils the entire evening for me. And traffic is unpredictable. The other night I practically had a heart attack when the movie was getting ready to start and we were twelve blocks away in heavy, stop-and-go traffic."

My Takeaway

Think about what you have learned. What is the most important thing you will take from this chapter? What is your "action item"?

✠
✠ ✠
Prayer

Dear LORD, you have created an astonishing variety of plants and animals and people on this amazing and wonderful planet Earth. But sometimes that variety — those differences — cause difficulties in our relationships. Please help us to work through those differences and to bring harmony to our relationships. In Jesus' name we thank you and praise you. Amen.

✠

Afterword

As you have seen in the discussion of more than fifty proverbs in this book, the secret to a happy marriage is not difficult to understand in conception, but it can be quite a challenge to implement in practice.

All a couple needs to do is give up selfishness ("me, my way, mine), grow up in maturity (no more fights to hurt your spouse's feelings, and no more thin-skinned, chip-on-the-shoulder hypersensitivity), and work toward each other's happiness and growth.

Turn love into a verb by living kindness, embodying compassion, demonstrating teamwork, and pouring out forgiveness, in order that all may be committed to righteousness and goodness and peace.

Rejoice with those who rejoice, and weep with those who weep. Be of the same mind toward one another; do not be haughty in mind, but associate with the lowly. Do not be wise in your own estimation. Never pay back evil for evil to anyone. Respect what is right in the sight of all men. If possible, so far as it depends on you, be at peace with all men.
 — *Romans 12:15-18*

✝

Appendices

1. The Choice: Reshaping Your Behavior to Refresh Your Marriage
2. The Magic Words that Make Marriage Last
3. The Keys to Happiness
4. The Five Cruel Truths about Marriage for Brides
5. The Ten Commandments of Marriage
6. The Fundamental Needs of Husbands and Wives
7. For Further Reading
8. Overcoming the Vicious Cycle of Insecurity
9. Fallacies of Reasoning and Arguing
10. Five Secret Keys to a Happy Marriage

Appendix 1
The Choice: Reshaping Your Behavior to Refresh Your Marriage

This table lists behaviors that will result in happiness or unhappiness for you and your spouse. It's your choice.

Happiness	Unhappiness
compassionate	critical
kind	contradicting
encouraging	discouraging
humble	angry
gentle	negative
patient	unloving
forgiving	shaming
loving	selfish
supporting	combative
partnering	competitive
appreciative	argumentative
thankful	whining
sympathetic	blaming
faithful	demanding
serving	rejecting
pleasant	dominating
amiable	controlling
gracious	distrusting
giving	contemptuous
positive	cold
complimenting	thoughtless
uplifting	insulting
cheerful	sulking
generous	haughty
affirming	negating
listening	lecturing

Think about your relationship with your spouse and compare your behaviors with the behaviors listed in the two columns.

You can draw your own conclusions from the results. If you don't like what you realize, you know exactly what to do.

> How you behave toward your spouse is **a choice.**

☦

See that no one repays another with evil for evil, but always seek after that which is good for one another and for all people.
—1 Thessalonians 5:15

☦

Appendix 2
The Magic Words that Make Marriage Last

These Magic Words, presented in random order, can help keep your marriage healthy and happy. Say them regularly, whenever you speak to your spouse. They really work. (Note: Including the intensifier in the parentheses doubles the magic.)

I love you
I support you
I'm here for you
You're wonderful
Thank you (so much)
You did a great job
You are (absolutely) right
Forgive me
You're (so) smart
You can do it
I'm (really) sorry
Please
I agree (completely)
You're beautiful
I have (every) confidence in you
I was wrong
You are a (super) blessing to me
I forgive you
I'm (so) glad I married you
You make me happy
I appreciate you
I need you

Appendix 3
The Keys to Happiness

Also known as
The Keys to Marriage
The Keys to Lasting Relationships
The Rules for Resolving Conflicts

1. Honor God.
2. Humble Yourself.
3. Listen First.
4. Practice Patience.
5. Gain Understanding.
6. Reduce Expectations.
7. Be Thankful.
8. Change Yourself.
9. Always Forgive.
10. Help Others.
11. Be Truthful.
12. Be Kind.
13. Choose Carefully.
14. Avoid Shortcuts.
15. Live in Genuine Love.
16. Be Moderate.
17. Give Generously.
18. Make Peace.

Appendix 4
The Five Cruel Truths About Marriage for Brides

When women who have been married many years are asked what truths about marriage they had to realize in order to find happiness, these truths are often mentioned:

Cruel Truth of Marriage #1
You can't fix your spouse.
Whatever defects you perceive in your spouse, do not plan of "fixing" them after marriage. The only person you can fix is yourself.

Cruel Truth of Marriage #2
Your happiness is your own responsibility.
It's not your spouse's job to make you happy.

Cruel Truth of Marriage #3
Not all problems with your spouse can be solved.
Sometimes a problem can be reduced, delayed, or modified, but many problems must be endured.

Cruel Truth of Marriage #4
Resentment makes a marriage bitter, not better.
Resentment lengthens and worsens the hurt. Don't let your disappointments fester into resentments.

Cruel Truth of Marriage #5
Yes, your spouse is crazy. But the good news is that you can be cured.
Understand that men and women are different.

✝

Appendix 5
The Ten Commandments of Marriage

[Homily delivered at the marriage of the author]
[to his excellent wife]

Dearly Beloved, you are about to commit yourselves to each other for the rest of your lives. Think about it. Day after day, week after week, month after—you get the idea. Now, I'm sure you both want your marriage to be successful and rewarding, not just at first when you're young and energetic, but over the long haul. And, believe it or not, there are some things you should know—and probably already do know—that can help substantially to make your marriage successful. It's not the kind of car you drive, nor the house you live in, not the tools you own, and not even chocolate.

Whether or not your marriage brings richness to yourselves and to others, whether it grows stronger or weaker, warm or cold, depends largely on how you treat each other. It depends on whether you continue to show each other love and respect. That much is obvious, but what does it mean as a practical matter?

Just as God has given us the Biblical Ten Commandments, I thought I'd give you the Ten Commandments for Marriage. And just as God's ten were given as rules for producing happiness in life, so these ten should be thought of as rules to follow in order to have a happy and successful marriage. These truths represent the accumulated wisdom of many couples who learned them the hard way, through many struggles and conflicts.

So here they are, free of charge, though originally bought at a high cost. And since we are in an entertainment age, I've arranged them in countdown order.

NUMBER TEN

Sooner or later, one of you is going to leave the other's favorite ice cream on the kitchen counter, causing a melted mess. Or one of you will forget to put gas in the car just before the other needs to drive far away for a meeting. Or one of you is going to lose the camera's little memory card, together with all the photos you took on your last vacation. You will be upset.

Instead of giving your spouse a verbal beating, however, put the event in the context of your life, your spouse's life, and your permanent relationship. And obey

The Tenth Commandment of Marriage:

10. Thou shalt chill out.

Let it go. Don't cry over spilled milk (or melted ice cream), especially when your spouse was the last person on the scene. Don't wait to find out by experience that it's not worth it to hurt your spouse over such ultimately insignificant mistakes. And besides, they are called accidents, not on-purpose-idents.

God's word tells us about number ten:

✝📖✝
Love bears all things and endures all things.
—1 Corinthians 13:7

NUMBER NINE

Remember the melted ice cream from number ten? Well, you shouldn't.

The Ninth Commandment of Marriage is,

9. Thou shalt forgive and forget.

This is an important idea because some people have a tendency to keep and nurture a grudge list of all the wrongs their spouse has committed against them during their entire marriage (and some overachievers include crimes committed against them during their dating time), so that whenever they get into an argument over something really important like forgetting to mail the gas bill or not refilling the salt shaker, they can call up their well-memorized list—sometimes it's more of a book than a list—and recite it in that special tone of voice some of you may be familiar with.

The message such a recital sends, of course, is that you were just kidding when you said you forgave your spouse for all those misdeeds and that you never really have gotten over the hurts they caused. If that's really the case, you have a lot to talk through, such as why that broken jar of pickles was so traumatic that you have never forgotten it, and more importantly, why you are weaponizing your spouse's innocent accidents.

God's word on this is that

✝📖✝

Love is patient and kind
it is not arrogant or rude
it is not irritable or resentful.
—1 Corinthians 13:4-5

> *Be on your guard! If your brother sins, rebuke him;*
> *and if he repents, forgive him.*
> *And if he sins against you*
> *seven times a day,*
> *and returns to you seven times, saying, "I repent,"*
> *forgive him.*
>
> —Luke 17:3-4

NUMBER EIGHT

We all know that hurtful words spoken in anger can never be completely erased from the mind of the target. Insults burrow deep. That's the power of language. But there is an upside. There are some Magic Words that can also burrow deep and help build up your spouse, cover over hurts, and strengthen your relationship.

The Eighth Commandment of Marriage is,

8. Thou shalt use the Magic Words.

I know these words are obvious, and I don't want to sound like a summer rerun, but for the sake of those who have not yet mastered the art of relationship building, here is a sample list. (A longer list appears in Appendix 2.)

The Magic Words

I love you	I agree completely
Thank you	I was wrong
You are right	You have my support
Forgive me	I forgive you
I'm sorry	Please

And a final comment on using these magic words. **More than half of the meaning of spoken words comes from the tone of voice of the speaker.** So remember to use the magic words with magic in your voice.

The Biblical truth here is from Proverbs:

✝📖✝

A soft answer turns away wrath,
But a harsh word stirs up anger.

And even more to the point,

A gentle tongue is a tree of life.
—Proverbs 15:1, 4a

NUMBER SEVEN

Ever hear someone tell their spouse, "You're not the person I married"? Men especially, but sometimes women too, need to understand that the togetherness of marriage not only means sharing the wonderful experiences of life together, but it also means physically—and occasionally mentally—falling apart together.

Age and gravity are not kind to anyone, and both partners should expect that their good looking spouse is eventually going to wrinkle, plump up, shed hair, and generally come to look like their grandparents.

The **Seventh Commandment of Marriage** is:

7. Thou shalt expect change.

Physical decline is only one kind of change you're likely to see in your spouse over time. Taste in food, entertainment, personal habits, likes and dislikes—all are subject to modification as time goes on.

The Biblical truth here is:

✝📖✝

Enjoy life with the woman whom you love
all the days of your fleeting life
which He has given to you under the sun;
for this is your reward in life
and in your toil in which
you have labored under the sun.
—Ecclesiastes 9:9

NUMBER SIX
The Sixth Commandment of Marriage is:

6. Thou shalt not expect change.

Seems like a contradiction with number seven, doesn't it? Ah, but that's often the way true wisdom works. Commandments Seven and Six form a paradox, which can be resolved thusly. Some people see their spouse as a remodeling project, assuming that after marriage they can bring in the tools and change whatever they don't like about the person they just married. If you're not happy with the way your spouse or spouse-to-be is right now, then you need to change **yourself**. That's a whole lot easier than changing the other person.

And where should you start in changing yourself? Start by accepting your spouse and those things you want him or her to change. That way, you can stop wanting to change them. Remember, a nag is a useless horse. So the wisdom here is, To change your spouse, change yourself first.

The Biblical truth here is,

✝📖✝
Love does not insist on its own way.
—1 Corinthians 13:5

NUMBER FIVE

The next commandment can be illustrated by a couple of observations. Recently at Home Depot, a woman said rather heatedly, "Where were you? I've been looking all over for you!" Yes, sometimes the kids need to be scolded, when they wander off. But in this case, the woman was talking to her husband. The second scene took place in Albertson's grocery store, where a married couple was shopping. One spouse said, "Let's get this raspberry jelly. It's good." To which the other replied rather forcefully, "Well, that would be for you. I don't like it and I won't eat any of it. But if you insist, go ahead and buy it."

Now excuse me if I don't understand, but what's the upside in either of these cases? Is either spouse going to end up happier as a result of this behavior? I mean, how reasonable or helpful is it to scold a man (in public!) for wandering off in Home Depot? Or for getting all snotty over a jar of jelly?

The fact is, you are going to be just about as happy — or unhappy — as your spouse is.

So, **The Fifth Commandment of Marriage** is:

5. Thou shalt make thyself happy by making thy spouse happy.

The Biblical admonition relevant here is,

✝📖✝

Let each one of you husbands love his wife as himself, and let the wife see that she respects her husband.
—Ephesians 5:33

Well, we're halfway through and we still haven't had a "thou shalt not," and marriage, like the rest of life, has a few don'ts that are needed for happiness together.

Number Four

You're going to marry a real person, which means an imperfect person, who is unlikely to remedy any of those imperfections. Too often people fall in love, not with another person, but with their own imagination projected onto some random passerby. They begin to attribute to the one they are dating all kinds of characteristics that the person really doesn't have. They see their short-tempered, cheapskate friend with no social skills as good natured, generous, and gregarious because that's what they want in a person. So they marry their imagination instead of the person at the altar with them.

Then, when they wake up with reality snoring next to them, it's not just disappointment that sets in, but resentment. The difference between the personality they imagined and the person burping loudly that they actually married produces a sense of injustice, a feeling of righteous indignation, even betrayal in the mind of the expecter, leading to conflict, nagging, and general recrimination.

The truth is, your spouse is only a mere human being, with unique qualities, tastes, habits, and preferences that mostly differ from those of your imaginary hero. Your spouse is not going to solve all your problems, fulfill you in every way, grant your every wish, or behave only the way you want. In fact, he or she might not even like the TV shows you like.

So, **The Fourth Commandment of Marriage** is:

4. Thou shalt not expect a perfect spouse.

That's the King James translation. The Contemporary English Version of this commandment is, "Get real." Of course, every couple about to marry agrees that they don't expect perfection, but in actual fact many do expect their spouse to measure up, to—themselves. It is said that in life in general we judge everything by our own experience, by the standard of Me. So in marriage, many spouses view as defects all the differences from their own preferences or habits. They think, "That's not the way I would do it, so it's wrong. Furthermore, I expect it to be done the way I would do it."

But your spouse not only has a distinctive set of behaviors, attitudes and habits, as I mentioned in the previous commandment, but he or she is the owner and exhibiter of just a truckload of flaw—I mean unique characteristics. But study the happy marriages and you'll find not that there are no irritants. The husband still blows his nose too loud, leaves his sweaty T-shirt on the bathtub, and puts the dirty dishes in the sink instead of the dishwasher. The wife is still always late getting ready for church, forgets to lock the front door, and continues to lose the caps on all the ball point pens in the house. But they are happy because they not only tolerate but they accept each other's distinctives. Some people call it love.

As the saying goes, "Blessed are the flexible, for they shall not be broken."

In other words, happiness in marriage comes—at least in part—from narrowing the distance between what you expect and what you get. Stay open to goodness in disguise: shortcomings and disappointments can turn into blessings.

The Biblical comment comes from the apostle Paul:

✝📖✝

And we know that for those who love God all things work together for good.
—Romans 8:28

Final comment on Commandment Four: A very old blessing given to many young marrieds by their elderly relatives is, "Husbands, be glad that your wife has so many flaws, for they are what kept her from getting a better husband; and wives, be glad that your husband has so many flaws, for they are what kept him from getting a better wife."

NUMBER THREE

The next Commandment is quite important because not only is it a major key to all types of interpersonal happiness but it is also the one that's broken most often, even though failure to follow it causes millions of couples to live together miserably. Okay, so—

The Third Commandment of Marriage is

3. Thou shalt get over thyself.

Yes, the golden key to happiness in marriage is the very same as the golden key to happiness in life, the realization that *it's not about you*.

In other words, happiness and joy belong to those who put the focus of their lives on someone or something other than themselves. Getting over yourself means calling on a sense of humility, and humility is excellent in a marriage. And for a truly happy marriage, it's a necessity.

Too many people enter a romantic relationship for what they think they can get out of it. And being self-focused, they enter the selfishness whirlpool: "I've been thinking of myself and what's in it for me, but I'm still not happy, so I need to be even more self-centered." For those who are thinking, "But life *is* all about me," I'm telling you, pride is a drunk driver who will never get you to the corner of Harmony and Bliss. And if you really think life is all about you, then when kids come along, the truth will hit you like a speeding cement truck sliding across the ice.

Some philosopher or other once commented on the benefits of taking yourself off your personal throne by noting, "The more you get, the more you have. The more you give, the more you are."

And Scripture supports this:

✝📖✝
*When pride comes, then comes disgrace,
but with the humble is wisdom.*
—Proverbs 11:2

So if you really want to be happily married, put your ego on a diet and lose the fat of selfishness.

After the shock from the third commandment of marriage has diminished a little, you must be curious and eager—and a little nervous—to find out what the two most important commandments are. So, here we go.

NUMBER TWO
The **Second Commandment of Marriage** is,

> **2. Thou shalt follow the Leader.**

This commandment for happiness follows from the previous one. Once you can get over yourself, you will realize that to have a successful marriage, you must follow the leader.

For husbands, this means submitting to the leadership of Christ as head of the marriage. In practical terms, this means prayerfully following Biblical principles in your relationship with your wife and in your decision making.

For wives, following the leader means deferring to your husband as head of the household. In practical terms, this means accepting control of the domains where you are better at than your husband is (keeping track of the budget? keeping the social calendar?), as well as helping him in decision making and being an agreeable and supportive partner in the marriage.

The Apostle Paul sums up this relationship in the Bible: "For the husband is the head of the wife even as Christ is the head of the church…. " And Paul continues, "Husbands, love your wives, as Christ loved the church and gave himself up for her. In the same way husbands should love their wives as their own bodies. He who loves his wife loves himself." —Ephesians 5:22-28

So, why is this a principle of happiness in marriage?

The simple fact is that without it, there is a very strong likelihood that husband and wife will engage in a struggle for domination that can destroy their happiness. Sometimes this struggle produces shouting, door-slamming arguments, but more often it's evidenced by little cutting remarks, criticisms, disagreements, sarcasm, and often disrespecting the spouse in front of other people. And the saddest part of this story is that frequently no one wins the struggle, so it continues for years, as the marriage grows weaker and weaker, ever more unhappy.

NUMBER ONE

And this brings us to **The First Commandment for Happiness in Marriage**.

I've just recommended getting over yourself and deferring to someone other than yourself for leadership. So what could be the most important commandment for marital happiness? That's the one commandment that empowers the other nine, and it's this:

1. Thou shalt put God first.

God has given us free will, which allows us to make our own choices. And we make the choices we do because we think that each choice will make us happier or at least less unhappy. As one philosopher noted, the desire for happiness is "the impulse behind all human actions," even those who choose to take drugs, get in fights, rob banks — or in the tamer arena of married life — argue, disrespect their spouse, give the silent treatment, or even rebel and have an affair. In both life and marriage, people often make poor choices in behavior because they are thinking of themselves at the moment.

But God has designed us and he knows what will increase our happiness and what will decrease it. And he has told us how to increase it — namely, by getting over ourselves and by following the leader in Christ. Putting God first and living according to his precepts in the Bible therefore means making better choices — choices that really do lead to happiness.

So, you see, these ten commandments of marriage, like the original Ten, are designed to bring joy into your marriage. And God knows how to help you put him first. Perhaps you are tired of bickering or else you fear that if you do marry, your life will be filled with squabbling and prideful silent treatments. Put God in charge of your life and follow these ten commandments for marriage and you'll see what a difference that makes.

There you have them. Think these over, and, if you really do want a great relationship, put them into practice.

✝

Appendix 6
The Fundamental Needs of Husbands and Wives in Marriage

I believe that the single most horrible problem for marriages today is the lack of understanding, not only of what is needed by a man in a woman but also what is needed by a woman in a man.
—Laura Schlessinger, *The Proper Care and Feeding of Marriage*, page 2

A major reason that men and women so often do not get along well in marriage is that even though each spouse's wants, needs, and priorities are very different, the husband assumes that his wife has the same wants and needs that he does, to the same degree; and the wife assumes that her husband has the same wants and needs that she does, to the same degree.

A second reason for the disharmony between spouses is that neither spouse discusses these differences. Even though these differences involve fundamental needs, the spouses are too shy or too embarrassed or too afraid of being criticized or shamed or even rejected if they admit to these needs. So they talk about something else.

The final reason for marital disharmony is that, even though some men and women will read this appendix or otherwise know what their spouse's fundamental needs are, they will be unwilling to supply them because they are unwilling to make the effort, to serve their spouse humbly, or to give up control.

Here, then, are the needs so seldom discussed between spouses, especially before marriage or in the first months or years. Regardless of your stage in life, whether married or single, if you want to improve your relationship, clarify your needs to each other with some serious discussion.

Husbands

The first secret is that men are simple creatures. Give a man a beer (or a soft drink) and a bowl of chips or popcorn, and he's good for three hours sitting in front of a giant screen TV, even by himself—no conversation necessary—even if a few friends are present.

> *It has been reliably reported that during a three-and-a-half-hour football game, a total of five words were spoken between the two men watching:*
>
> *"Want another beer?"*
> *"Sure. Thanks."*
>
> *When asked how they spent their afternoon, they said, quite simply, "We watched the game and talked."*

Once women understand this straightforward, unpretentious simplicity, they will be a little less surprised to learn how basic a husband's needs are that he wants his wife to supply. The top three:

Conjugation

Well, to be blunt, men need frequent sex in a hungry, almost desperate way, but they seldom discuss this fact with their fiancé before marriage because they are afraid that their bride-to-be will think they are some kind of twisted, uncouth sex pervert and break off the engagement. New wives are often shocked at this need. "All he wants is sex," they tell their girlfriends. That's almost right.

Recommendation 1: *Give your husband all the sex he wants.* Unless you are actually ill, don't reject his need. If you are tired or not in the mood, remember that often both you and he go to work, do chores, and take care of the kids when you are tired and not in the mood and would rather just go to sleep. If you go to work out of duty even though you are tired, shouldn't you accommodate your husband out of love even though you are tired?

> **Give your husband all the sex he wants.**

Just think that what is a slight inconvenience to you to give to your husband is a significant comfort and blessing to him to receive. So, "Let him have his way with you." He will be deeply grateful and think you are the best wife in the world. Many, if not most, of your other marital problems will shrink or disappear altogether if you follow this recommendation. And your bonding together will grow stronger and stronger.

By the way, this advice is very Biblical:

Rejoice in the wife of your youth. As a loving hind and a graceful doe, Let her breasts satisfy you at all times; Be exhilarated always with her love. — Proverbs 5:18b-19

Husbands and wives should be fair with each other about having sex. A wife belongs to her husband instead of to herself, and a husband belongs to his wife instead of to himself. So don't refuse sex to each other, unless you agree not to have sex for a little while, in order to spend time in prayer. — 1 Corinthians 7:3-5a (CEV)

In a word, then, relax and enjoy your husband's demonstration of his love and care for you, and his enjoyment of your body. And he will be strengthened and encouraged by your gracious accommodation of his needs.

Recommendation 2: *Never use sex as a weapon.* Both granting sex as a reward and withholding sex as a punishment are harmful to the relationship because weaponizing sex makes it into an object of transaction and manipulation, not a sharing of love and pleasure. And seeing sex as a commodity might cause your husband to view you as a commodity.

How blessed is the husband who can say, "We've been married for many years and we've had a few arguments, but I've never had to spend a night on the sofa."

Cooking

There is a little Ozzie and Harriet idealization in most men, especially as it concerns making food. Yes, this is old fashioned and probably sexist, but if you prepare food that your husband likes, he will not only be happier, but he will brag to his buddies about how wonderful you are.

> **Serve good food
> And your husband will serve you for life.**

Note that the operative term here is *prepare*, not *cook*. Husbands are glad to have healthy (and sometimes otherwise) food, made available by their loving wives, even though it was purchased from a fast-food establishment, a wholesale warehouse, or an online, ingredients-to-you business.

The food doesn't have to be fancy. Most men love cheeseburgers, tacos, burritos, fish sandwiches, Italian foot-longs, barbecue anything—simple and straightforward. For most men, a well-made sandwich is better than prime rib. It's the idea that you are thinking about his food needs and taking care of them that is important. Provide a variety for him. Don't refuse to cook bacon. Do cook healthy food, but stop with the tofu.

Confidence

Many men are at least somewhat confident in their role as knowledge workers, whether in their job (architect, automobile repairman, fireman, policeman, teacher) or in their homeowner role (gardener, plumber, electrician, painter). But when it comes to relations with their wives, most men are much more sensitive than they appear, equipped as thy are with very fragile, egg-shell egos and a profound lack of understanding about women. In addition to men's natural self-doubt, their wives sometimes tell them (or imply by criticism) that they don't measure up to expectations—so they feel like broken failures.

To have a happy husband, study to be kind, approving, and supportive. Tell him how much you appreciate him. Praise him when he fixes something. When you meet after an absence, run up to him and give him a hug and a kiss. Be the first to give affection. Flatter him occasionally. Tell him, "I'm so glad you are here."

> **Men want to feel needed physically and respected emotionally by a woman.**

Tell him he is your hero and that you feel safe and secure when he is around. Kind words like these validate his life. A man wants to be valued and respected and needed, especially by his wife. Remind him that he is strong, and tell him he is "a real man." Comments like these will go a long way toward erasing the negative hype often directed at men.

And be happy. Husbands are notorious for blaming themselves when their wives mope around. Show him instead that you are actually happy with him, and find him the source of you cheerfulness. It's difficult to understate his resulting joy.

> **Count Your Blessings**
> If you have a habit of emphasizing the negative and downplaying the positive in your life or marriage, get a sheet of paper and start writing down your blessings. Food, shelter, transportation, entertainment, books to help you improve your marriage. . . .

Happiness (and gloominess) are contagious. Spread some joy around in your marriage. When it's important, act happy even though you don't feel happy. If you can't fake it, explain your sorrow, prefixed by telling him that he's not the cause of it.

Any wife who makes a consistent effort to fulfill these primary needs of her husband (informally known as "Sex, Sandwiches, and Support") will find a much happier, more cooperative, helpful, loving husband.

Wives

The overarching truth about women that men do not know is that women are much more complex than men. Most husbands will need a lifetime to understand their wives. Their wives will probably wonder about this. Here are three of the most fundamental needs wives want to have supplied by their husbands.

Love and Emotional Connection

There's a reason women read all those romance novels and watch all those Hallmark movies. They are obsessed with being loved, which, unlike men, is more emotional than physical, although the physical certainly plays a part.

> **The need to feel loved is the first fundamental need of a wife.**

One of women's great desires is to be wanted. Women need reassurance that they are now and forever loved—that is, valued, desired, esteemed, and—yes—treasured.

The sad fact is, most men have an uncanny ability to make their wives feel taken for granted. To help remedy this, demonstrate your love by a (more than momentary) hug, a kiss, a note, a flower, anything that shows you are thinking of her and appreciate her. (But don't try a DustBuster or a Weight Watcher's gift card for Christmas.) A warm comment in a warm tone will melt her heart. So show your affection, regularly. Kiss and caress her sometimes when you *aren't* trying to warm her up for sex, but just want to show affection.

> **Give your wife a lot of time and attention to make her feel wanted and valued.**

I know it is difficult, but *listen to your wife*. Yes, she will go on and on, and provide you with way too many details—and she will repeat them, both in different words and in the same words. But she does this to build your relationship with her—and, frankly, to see what she thinks. Men ponder the pro and con quietly, and deliver their conclusion aloud at the end. Women explore a decision in public space, talking, often at length, through alternatives, reasons, evidence, conclusions, and so on right in the hearing of anyone they trust.

Ask questions; show that you are interested in your wife's deliberations, her inner life, and outer challenges.

Unless she clearly asks for your advice, avoid saying, "Well, here's what you should do about that." Just listen.

Interconnectedness

Yes, just listen, even if you don't quite get what is going on. For women, everything is interconnected emotionally. Husbands need to realize that what to them would be a shift in subject is to their wives only the exploration of another connection.

And this is a significant challenge to a husband's understanding of his wife. Women join all their thoughts, experiences, doubts, plans, fears, and analyses together in an interconnected, holistic consciousness—that they explore by talking aloud. It seems that women's brains are much less lateralized than men's, allowing for a staggering number of connections between ideas. While men tend to think in boxes (which they then line up in straight lines), women "think all over their brains."

Activity

Divide into opposite sex pairs (such as husband and wife) or quads (two husbands and two wives) and read the story below.

Everything Is Interconnected

Herb and his girlfriend Helen spent the day at an amusement park riding a few rides, eating some cotton candy and talking about nothing in particular. Both had talked animatedly for much of the day, but Helen had become almost silent for the last hour or two.

Herb finally noticed Helen's reticence, and, after checking his watch, thought it might be due to her hunger.

"Shall we go to The Cave," Herb began, "that quiet little restaurant across the way, where we can sit close to each other and cuddle while we eat?"

Instead of grabbing Herb's arm, looking warmly into his eyes, and saying "Yes" lovingly, Helen said, in a surprisingly hostile tone of voice, "I don't know how you can ask that after what happened today."

Surprised and confused, Herb asked, "What happened today?"

"Don't act as if you don't know," Helen said, sternly.

"But Helen, Sweetheart, I really don't know. Did I do something wrong?"

"When you taunted that lion at Zooland and it roared at you, I was terribly frightened. I thought it was going to jump out of the pen and attack you."

"Oh, that wasn't dangerous," Herb answered. "Besides, I didn't realize that the roaring lion upset you so much."

"Well, you should have," Helen said, just about coming to tears. "I've been thinking about it ever since. And now you've made it even worse."

"I have?" Herb was even more surprised.

"Yes," Helen said. "By asking me to dinner as if nothing happened when my feelings are so hurt."

Discuss the story, focusing on whether the men and women in your group understand Herb and Helen's response to the events.
1. Do the men understand Helen's response?
2. Do the women understand Herb's confusion?
3. Ask if anyone would like to share an example of a similar disconnect between husband and wife (or boyfriend and girlfriend). Explain how the misunderstanding occurred, what difficulty it caused, and how it was resolved.

Safety and Security

Because men are bigger and stronger and not necessarily wiser than women, men are generally less fearful of their physical environment than women are. Therefore, men don't understand that a strong priority for most women is safety and security. Women want—no, they need—to be protected and cared for in a way that makes them feel safe. Women are nest builders, not wandering hunters (the way men often see themselves) and they want their homes to be places where they can feel safe and be safe to raise their children.

> **Both financial and physical security are important to women.**

Security includes financial security (a commitment to providing the necessities of life for the woman and her children) and emotional security (permanent commitment to the relationship and to the family).

When a husband provides a safe, comfortable living space for his wife and family (a house that she can turn into a home), and when he is careful to feed the family savings and investments for the future, he makes her feel both loved and secure.

> **Save Money: Avoid Insecurity**
> A recent government study revealed that 40% of Americans have less than $400 saved to meet any kind of emergency.

Predictability and Rationality

Some men like to pretend that women are purely emotional beings, always changing their minds based on feelings, making irrational decisions, and so forth. But such a prejudice shows how little such men know about women's inner life, and underscores how crucial it is that husbands take time to understand their wives.

Many husbands are surprised to discover, shortly after marriage, that they have landed in the middle of a war between themselves and their wives—a war for dominance and control, with a person they love deeply. Sometimes, when both spouses are strong willed, the battle can rage for years. Usually, however, because most men are emotionally vulnerable to their wives, the wife soon "rules the relationship and the home,"[12] controlling the social calendar, division of labor, and so on.

Wives are really the rule keepers (and rule makers) in most marriages. They want their lives to follow a set of predictable, sensible rules that will enable them to live orderly, happy and stable lives.

That's why so many wives want to be in charge. If the wife calls the shots, so to speak, she thinks that she can establish and maintain control and keep her husband off balance and therefore less of a threat.

And that's why so many newlywed husbands are often so surprised to discover that their brides have already composed a rather lengthy and incredibly elaborate rule book: where the scissors go, which brand of laundry detergent to use, exactly how to wash the casserole pan, which chemical cleaner to use on which surface, where the unopened and opened mail goes, how the furniture pillows need to be arranged, and so on.

> **Work out the practical household rules together. Don't be overly obsessive.**

Complying with the wife's rules can be a challenge for the new husband because
- There are many rules.
- The rule book is not in writing but exists only in the wife's mind.

---

[12] Laura Schlessinger, *The Proper Care and Feeding of Marriage*, page 99.

- Wives typically expect the husband to know the rules from the beginning of the marriage.
- The rules are subject to change without notice.

In the following vignette, notice how the wife's control of the rules also helps keep her in control of her husband:

Lost and Found

Ted: "Jane, sweetheart, where are the scissors I was using this morning? I left them right here."

Jane: "Ted, darling. I put them back."

Ted: "Where might that be, Jane, dear?"

Jane: "I put them back right where they belong."

Ted: "And where is that, my love?"

Jane: "Don't cross me, Ted. You know very well where the scissors belong."

Ted: "Um, could you remind me again?"

Jane: "Honestly! You men! What's wrong with you, anyway? As if I exist to tell you where everything belongs!"

Trouble in Wedlock

Women's nature—including the desire for safety, security, predictability, and rationality—enables them to be highly effective as organizers and directors. And, of course, as mothers. We have all felt great admiration seeing a woman taking charge of a civic organization, her workgroup at the office, the school children's musical, and so forth, and even greater admiration when they raise their kids.

Women generally task-switch[13] faster and more efficiently than men.

But these attributes can create challenges in marriage. The fundamental needs we have been discussing almost irresistibly push wives to want control in the marriage and dominance over their husbands. Realizing that they are physically weaker than the men they marry, many women attempt (and often succeed) to control their husbands by "taking them down a notch," through emotional manipulation. Women's natural verbal advantage allows them to talk their husbands into submission.

What do wives want? Control.

Unfortunately, keeping the husband off balance emotionally is not the way to build a happy life — for husband or wife. If, up to this point, you have wondered why this book covers so many proverbs warning about critical, nagging, contentious wives, you should understand now. Wives managing the household economy need to be careful to act in loving, soft, gentle ways and to negotiate and compromise. If a husband feels a positive warmth from his wife, he will accept her plans much more readily.

---

[13] Task switching used to be called multitasking, until it was demonstrated that the brain is changing between tasks rapidly, not performing more than one task at the same time.

In addition to setting and enforcing the operational ground rules for the home, the wife usually controls the emotional character of the marriage, thereby controlling her husband's mood. (That's where the saying, repeated often in this book, "Happy wife, happy life" originated: a happy wife spreads joy throughout her house, while an unhappy wife brings her husband—and her entire home—down.)

By a combination of complaint, criticism, nagging, anger, crying, yelling, withholding sex, arguing, being glum, and giving the silent treatment (for days if necessary), many women have learned that they can get their husbands to do just about anything the wife wants.

In response to one of her callers who used the excuse that her husband agreed to let her visit her parents for a month, marriage therapist Dr. Laura Schlessinger said,

> Husbands will agree to anything we want just to keep us happy and having sex with them. You know that. You know that he agrees to all sorts of things just to make sure that you're okay with him and he doesn't get punished.[14]

Sadly, few marriages operated in this way are happy marriages. The husbands feel henpecked, broken, rejected, unloved and disrespected; and the wives can grow arrogant, contemptuous, and resentful—for they eventually come to believe that they can't respect a man

---

[14] *The Proper Care and Feeding of Marriage*, page 217

whom they must constantly criticize and correct and dominate.

> **You will find what you look for.**
> **If you look for your husband's faults,**
> **you will find an endless number.**
> **If you look for his virtues and strengths,**
> **you will find an endless number.**

The Big Question

The question is, then, how can the fundamental needs of wives (love and emotional connection, safety and security, and predictability and rationality) be fulfilled by their husbands when it is the wives' own tendency to take control, often by using emotional manipulation, that inhibits the ability or desire of their husbands to provide those very things? How can this tendency be replaced in favor of the positive models presented in this book? How can both husbands and wives find joy, fulfillment, and mutual love together in marriage?

The Author's Relevant Anecdote

When I taught critical thinking to college students, I included a segment where we analyzed advertising appeals. We discussed some of the techniques marketers use to make their products more appealing.

One such advertisement from a magazine showed a beautiful sailboat with the sails fully unfurled. On the deck was a woman holding on to the large, round steering wheel. Close behind her was a man, with one hand on her shoulder and the other hand pointing in the direction they were sailing.

What the picture said to the women students produced such a profound effect on them that they became somewhat emotional. The picture resonated with their fundamental needs to feel in control and yet feel secure and safe and loved by a man. Some of the students referred to the picture in future class sessions, saying how powerfully it worked on them, even though they were not interested in buying a sailboat or the product being advertised, which I have forgotten.[15]

The Big Answer

The big answer, then, that will make both spouses feel fulfilled and happy, is to construct a marriage based on mutually empowering, rewarding, loving, and respecting principles. Follow these steps, adopt these principles, live in the new way you have learned in this book and in the methods below, and you will be able to improve your life, your spouse's life, your marriage, and your service to all.

Note that none of these principles are easy. Some are quite challenging. None of these can be forced upon you. You must choose voluntarily—and, let us hope, cheerfully—to practice these behaviors, just as you intentionally

---

[15] Semiotics is the study of how pictures and objects present meanings beyond the surface appearance, like the man, woman, and steering wheel here.

choose your tone of voice and attitude when you interact with others.

1. Change the focus of your life from taking to giving. It seems that most people are interested in getting what they can out of life and out of other people, without much thought of what they want to give back. In other words, their thought and speech and actions are all about me, me, me. This is especially true in marriage.

> **Change the focus of your life
> From Taking to Giving**

But did it ever occur to you that the most selfish people are the least happy? They think, "I've thought only of myself in this relationship and taken what I'm entitled to whenever I could. But I'm still not happy. That means I need to be even more selfish and take, take, take for me, me, me even more."

And how's that working for you? Not good, eh? Isn't it the most generous (and kindest) people who are the happiest?

And you guessed it. This is another way of saying "Humble yourself." Until you get control over your own ego, life will be difficult, unhappy, and increasingly lonely. Instead of forcing your ego to feed off of innocent others or to measure yourself by greedy "conquests," become a servant and help those who have need.

> **Stop being thoughtless and self-centered.**

It's so difficult because this behavior requires not a simple change of choices, not just an attitude revision, but a personality transplant, a spiritual renewal, right down to the core of your being. You no longer work just for your benefit, but for the benefit of others, in this order: serving God, your spouse, your children, your parents, your friends, your brothers and sisters in the faith, and so on. And it is service, sometimes, at great cost:

> *"Calling them to Himself, Jesus said to them, 'You know that those who are recognized as rulers of the Gentiles lord it over them; and their great men exercise authority over them.*
>
> *But it is not this way among you, but whoever wishes to become great among you shall be your servant; and whoever wishes to be first among you shall be slave of all. For even the Son of Man did not come to be served, but to serve, and to give His life a ransom for many.'"*
> — Mark 10:42-45

Yes, changing the focus of your life might just necessitate giving your life for another. If you live with this fact, this commitment, in mind, you will treat your spouse with great love and firm respect, knowing the responsibility you have for your spouse's safety and protection.

Activity
Discuss each of these proverbs. Have you found them to be true in your own observation and experience?

1. The more you get, the more you have. The more you give, the more you are.
2. The way to be happy is to give yourself away.
3. If you have a bad heart, maybe you need an attitude transplant.
4. Happiness and misery are both choices.
5. Change your behavior, change your life.
6. Be kind, be happy.

2. Face Conflict, Disagreement, and Misunderstanding with Love and Grace. As difficult as it is to remember when you crash into an issue with your spouse, your marriage is a partnership with someone you love and care for, and for whom you want happiness, prosperity, and all things good.

Problems should be viewed as opportunities to be creative together, not as occasions for hostility and anger.

In the unlikely case that you have read through this book and worked through its instructions, but have still not quite gotten on board with its philosophy, here is one more case for you to study:

Story for Discussion
Read the following story in your study group or as a husband and wife pair and discuss. Then answer the questions at the end.

TYPICAL SPAT CREATES HEAT BUT NO WARMTH
Gale: "Where do you think you are going, Bill?"
Bill: "I'm going to the golf course to hit a few balls."

Gale: "No, you're not. Put that golf bag down and get that bucket and the spray wash. You're going to clean the driveway."

Bill: "But I have to meet Arnie and Mike. They are expecting me."

Gale: "That's too bad. Call them and tell them your wife wants you to clean the driveway."

Bill: "The driveway can wait. My time with the guys is important."

Gale: "There will be lots of other opportunities for you to waste time and money on golf or some other frivolous thing. Here. I'm calling Mike for you now."

Bill: "Tell Mike I'm heading for the golf course. I'll be back around 7 or 8 this evening."

Gale: "Fine. I'll put your pillow and a blanket on the sofa for you. And you can get your own breakfast, too."

Discussion Questions

1. Characterize Bill and Gale. What attitudes define each one?
2. How do the chosen interactive styles of each spouse help create and maintain their marriage relationship?
3. Think about the goal of Bill's and Gale's comments. What seems to be the purpose of each spouse's comments?
4. Do you think the purpose will be fulfilled by the things the couple say to each other?
5. How desirable a mate is Gale? Is Bill? Explain why.
6. Do you think Bill and Gale are happy? Why or why not?
7. Do you think Bill and Gale would like to be happy with each other?
8. Is there a better way for Bill or Gale to handle this situation?

"New" Activity

Now pretend that Bill and Gale have been processed through an Attitude Changer (Model Presto X-1).

Here is a transcript of their interaction based on their new attitudes.

HEARTWARMING CONFLICT

NewGale: "Hey, Bill. If I were Sherlock Holmes, noticing your golf bag over your shoulder and your golf shoes and car keys in your hands, I would conclude that you are heading to the golf course."

NewBill: "Your conclusion would be correct, my dear. That's why I love you so much. You are so smart."

NewGale: "You love me because I'm smart? And here I thought your affection was pinned to my Triple Chocolate Decadence Suicide Cake."

NewBill: "Well, there's a lot to love about you, Sweetheart."

NewGale: "And, um, you were going to tell me about this outing exactly when?"

NewBill: "I'm sure I told you about our plans right when the guys and I made them. It was Tuesday, I think."

NewGale: "Uh, yeah. That would be not. I've been planning for weeks for you to clean the driveway today."

NewBill: "I didn't tell you? In that case, another reason I love you is your cheery forgiveness for my stupid forgetting to let you know."

NewGale: [With mock seriousness] "So you really think I'm going to forgive you for this, do you?"

NewBill: "How about if I come home by five and do the driveway then?"

> *NewGale:* [With pretended reluctance] "Well, as much as I hate to compromise, I guess I can let it go this time."
>
> *NewBIll:* "Oh, thank you, thank you, Sweetheart. And you still love me, too?"
>
> *NewGale:* [with fake seriousness] "Don't push it, Bill."

Here you can see a possible source of argument has turned into a positive, playful, loving interchange that solved a problem quickly and effectively.

"New" Activity Discussion Questions

1. What differences do you see in the way Bill and NewBill and Gale and NewGale handle the issue?
2. What is the difference in focus between Gale and NewGale and between Bill and NewBill?
3. Do you think NewBill and NewGale are happy? Why or why not?
4. What, do you think, has caused NewBill and NewGale to interact this way?

Why not be a pleasant, kind spouse?
It takes little effort and you'll feel better, too.

---

3. Divide, Conquer, and Unite. To create an efficient, happy, effective marriage, plan its operating system before you are wedded. If you are already married, and perhaps have been for a long time, the same advice applies. Get together and discuss which spouse should be responsible for which of the various domains in the marriage. One spouse might be responsible for an entire domain, or the responsibility could be divided.

For example:

Finances: Cindy, weekly budget; Carlos, taxes (income tax, property tax, home insurance, automobile insurance, health insurance)

Housekeeping: Acme Maids, regular cleaning; Cindy, laundry; Carlos, everything outdoors and all mechanicals (washer, dryer, heating, air conditioning, plumbing, electrical)

Automobiles: Carlos, all

Food Provision: Cindy, Mon-Sun except Carlos Fri dinner, Sat lunch & dinner, Sun dinner

Gardening: Both

Of course, the initial task assignments should not be fixed in stone, but should be adjustable based on experience and continued discussion. Flexibility will enable spouses to respond to unexpected events or the increase or decrease in work required to maintain an area.

4. Follow the Biblical model.

Christians are a people under authority, with a specific position in the hierarchy of the Kingdom of God: God the Father is ruler over all; Jesus listens to the Father and does his will, and believers obey the teachings of Jesus.

For the family unit, the hierarchy of authority is that children are accountable to their parents (Colossians 3:20), the wives are accountable to their husbands (and to Christ), and the husbands are accountable to Christ.

> *But I want you to know that Christ is the head of every man, and the man is the head of the woman, and God is the head of Christ.*
> *— 1 Corinthians 11:3*
>
> *Wives, be subject to your own husbands, as to the Lord. For the husband is the head of the wife, as Christ also is the head of the church, He Himself being the Savior of the body.*
> *— Ephesians 5:22-23*

This means that the husband is ultimately responsible for the safety, security, predictability, and rationality of the marriage, as well as its spiritual health and growth. The hierarchy exists to make easier the creation of a harmonious, peaceful family, operating as a focused team, moving in one direction—toward the service and glory of God.

This framework empowers wives to find strength and the safe fulfillment of their fundamental needs, structured in a positive, productive, rewarding way. Instead of endeavoring to control her husband (and therefore the marriage) by using emotional manipulation, the wife can find joy participating in consensus building, compromise, trade-offs, moving the family forward—while supporting her husband and building a strong unity between him and herself.

With the Christian model, there is no room for competition, rebellion, antagonism, or using emotional or sexual weaponry. We are commanded not only to work as a team, but to love our teammates:

> *A new commandment I give to you, that you love one another, even as I have loved you, that you also love one another. By this all men will know that you are My disciples, if you have love for one another.*
> — John 13:34-35

In those rare cases where husband and wife differ over an issue and cannot resolve it with a compromise or a consensus solution, the wife is therefore to defer to her husband:

> *But as the church is subject to Christ, so also the wives ought to be to their husbands in everything.* — Ephesians 5:24

In return, as the leaders of the family unit, husbands are commanded to be obedient to Christ's teachings, treat their children well (Colossians 3:21) and love their wives, up to the point of dying for them:

> *Husbands, love your wives, just as Christ also loved the church and gave Himself up for her. . . . Nevertheless, each individual among you also is to love his own wife even as himself, and the wife must see to it that she respects her husband.*
> — Ephesians 5:25, 33

The truth becomes evident: A Christian husband, who loves his wife as he loves himself and is willing to die for her, and who puts Christ at the head of his life and marriage, who submits to the commandments of Christian behavior, will never become a dictator ordering his wife around. Instead, as already discussed, the family will most likely practice domain authority, where each spouse (and children, too, as the case may be) takes responsibility for specific domains in the family, making the ordinary decisions of household operation.

Appendix 6 Discussion Questions

1. One claim of this appendix is that a husband's top three needs from his wife are Conjugation, Cooking, and Confidence (also known as "Sex, Sandwiches, and Support"). Discuss each of these needs and say whether you think they are the top three needs that a husband expects his wife to fulfill.
2. Have husbands and wives pair up (two husbands to two wives) to discuss the husband's needs and how the wife should meet these needs. Discuss why some wives are unwilling to supply all three needs as described?
3. In the section under Wives, discuss each of these needs and say whether you think they are the top needs that a wife wants her husband to fulfil. (Recall that the needs are Love and Emotional Commitment, Safety and Security, and Predictability and Rationality — also known as "Compassion, Cash, and Control"). Discuss reasons husbands might fail to supply these listed needs of their wives.
4. **Husbands:** In the description of what wives need, the first item, Love and Emotional Connection, is rather abstract. Make a list of things you can do, say, or write that will let your wife know that you love her and enjoy feeling connected to her. Tell her what a blessing she is to you.

Wives: Think about the need for Confidence that men have. Make list of things you can do, say, or write that will make your husband feel confident in his role as a man and as your husband. Tell him how much you need him and how blessed you are to have him as your man.

Giver or Taker Activity

Discuss each of the following words and state how you respond to them: positively, negatively, neutrally. Do you find one category more appealing than the other? If so, explain why.

Give or Take?

Give	Take
obligation	entitlement
responsibility	liberty
requirement	rights
duty	privilege
task	autonomy
commitment	freedom
others	self

What does your response to the words in the table above tell you about current social attitudes? Do you think there are more Givers or more Takers in modern culture?

✟

Appendix 7
For Further Reading

There are many books covering relationships and how to make them lasting and happy. Rather than include an extensive (and daunting) bibliography, however, I wanted to offer readers a short but essential list of practical titles.

My recommendation is that every married couple, and anyone interested in getting married in the future, should read and discuss each of these books together and ask and think about and process all of the questions that arise.

It is my hope that you will read *Marriage in a Nutshell: Expanded Edition* first, of course, and with your significant other. You will be edified and encouraged.

Here, then, are the books I recommend:

John Gottman and Nan Silver. *The Seven Principles for Making Marriage Work.* **2nd ed., 2015.**
Gottman has developed seven principles for creating happy, loving marriages, derived from and reinforced by 43 years of laboratory observation, many randomized clinical trials and controlled studies, and interviews with and observations of tens of thousands of married couples.

John Gottman and Joan DeClaire. *The Relationship Cure.* **2001.**
This is an instructional book with attitude scales, designed for couples to work through

together to create a powerful, loving, solid relationship.

John Gray. *Men are from Mars, Women are from Venus.* 1992

A tremendous amount of misery has resulted from the claim that men and women are the same, except for social conditioning. Those who believe that will never understand the opposite sex. Fortunately, John Gray takes the understanding that has been learned from years of counseling and observation and presents it in an easy to grasp book.

Laura Schlessinger. *The Proper Care and Feeding of Husbands.* 2004.

Schlessinger describes the behaviors and attitudes that wives need to master, together with the behaviors and attitudes they need to avoid or stop, in order to make a happy and successful marriage. Why wives? The wife determines the emotional climate of the home in nearly all cases.

Gary Chapman, *The Five Love Languages*, 2015.

All people, Chapman says, have a need to feel loved, but there are five distinct methods ("languages") for conveying the message of "I love you." Each person conveys love using the language they prefer for themselves. For example, if John's love language is "getting gifts," he gives gifts to Sheila in order to convey the message that he loves her because that is the love language that works in his own heart.

However, if Sheila's love language is "verbal affirmation," the gifts will have much less impact than if John gave her cards and notes telling her what a smart, accomplished, desirable girl she is, because that is her love language.

Here is a paraphrased list of Chapman's five love languages. I have changed the actual language names so that you will be encouraged to buy and read this important book.

- verbal affirmation: support, encouragement, praise, gratitude
- time spent together: talking, playing a game, enjoying each other
- getting gifts: cards, tickets, books, whatever the person likes
- providing service: fix the garbage disposer, drive to the store
- physical connection: caressing, holding hands, making love

Laura Schlessinger. *The Proper Care and Feeding of Marriages.* **2007.**

In this follow-on book to *The Proper Care and Feeding of Husbands*, Schlessinger explores the damage to marriages caused by pride and selfishness, together with the remedies to the self-created misery so many marriages suffer from.

Willard F. Harley, Jr., *His Needs Her Needs.* **4th ed. 2011.**

Harley asks couples to rank the priority of importance for ten emotional needs:

admiration	financial support
affection	honesty and openness
conversation	physical attractiveness
domestic support	recreational companionship
family commitment	sexual fulfillment

His findings are that for many couples, "the five listed as most important by men were usually the five least important for women, and vice versa" (page 18).

These books, together with the book you are reading, *Marriage in a Nutshell: Expanded Edition,* will give you enormous insight into and understanding of romantic and interpersonal relationships.

(Note: I receive no compensation or other incentive for recommending these books.)

✝

Appendix 8
Overcoming the Vicious Cycle of Insecurity

THE CYCLE
The Partners Are Insecure. The problem begins with insecurity. One or both spouses feels as if they just don't measure up, to their spouse, their friends, to society.

The Partners Are Self-Focused. The spouses are both concerned about themselves, trying to avoid being ignored, taken for granted, ordered around, or stifled.

The Partners Engage in a Power Struggle. Each spouse strives to be the boss of the other, to assert their "rights."

The Partners Use Controlling Behaviors. One spouse might use anger as a controlling tactic, while the other might use silence, leave the room (or the house).

The Relationship Weakens. The weakening relationship increases insecurity and the cycle continues.

THE SOLUTION
Insecure Partners Change Focus. Instead of being concerned with themselves or with their partners, the spouses focus outside themselves. Insecurity from the threat of the other is reduced.

The Partners Become a Team. The spouses join together in a combined effort to accomplish specific goals for others.

The Partners Serve and Give Together. Spouses come to see each other as allies and not threats, enemies, or competitors.

The Relationship Strengthens and Insecurity Diminishes. Healing of the insecure self and bonding with spouse can take place.

THE KEY

Meet with your partner or spouse and follow these team-based problem solving steps.

A. Agree on what the problem is. Have each person state the problem, listen to the partner's statements of the problem, and then repeat back to the partner the partner's statement. Once you both agree on the problem statement, write it down and go to the next step.

B. Brainstorming together, identify the causes of the problem. Attempt to assign a weight to each cause. For example,
   a. Problem: Car ran out of gas
   b. Causes: (1) No one filled car up when needed (2) No one felt responsible for checking level and filling car when needed.

C. Identify and write down a solution. For example: Each driver must check gas gauge at startup. If gas level is one-quarter tank or below, tank should be filled ASAP.

Appendix 9
Fallacies of Reasoning And Arguing

Many times, when spouses (and other people) argue, they soon resort to using statements that are not fair or not relevant to the situation. For example, when they recognize that they are losing the argument, many arguers simply change the subject and start a different argument, one they think they can win.

What is the Purpose of Arguing?

When people are asked, "What is the purpose of argument?" more often than not the answer is, "To prove the other person wrong." That is the wrong answer. Unfortunately, that seems to be the answer many married couples give—and practice.

The purpose of argument is to find the truth, not to use your spouse as a punching bag. Notice that none of the terms below include the idea that the goal of an argument is to blame, punish, humiliate, shame, scorn, or inflict emotional damage on another person.

Discussion	An exchange of views and information
Dispute	A conflict over the truth of an idea
Argument	Presentation of evidence to persuade
Disagreement	Difference of belief or opinion

In order to help you remember that disagreements should be conducted with respect, kindness, and restraint, this appendix lists a few of the most common errors of reasoning (known as logical fallacies). To be fair and reasonable and logical, an argument must avoid all of these fallacies. When you disagree with your spouse, engage in a discussion that will calmly and fairly seek to find the truth or a resolution to the issue. Don't get into a shouting match where you can use your spouse as a punching bag, hitting "below the belt" with fallacious appeals.

1. You're guilty, too
This fallacy is one of the most common errors in argument. The fallacy is committed when one arguer defensively accuses the other of doing the same thing or something similar to the thing just criticized.

> *Joe: "You took money out of my wallet without telling me."*
> *Jane: "Well, you took my car to the bowling alley without asking me and used up half the gas."*

The problem with this kind of defensive response is that it shifts the argument away from the topic and onto another topic. In the example above, Joe must decide whether to change the topic to using his wife's car or to stay on the problem as first raised.

A similar defensive shift of argument occurs when the respondent says that the action being criticized is common, and therefore excusable.

> Gwen: "You didn't close and lock the window in the front room last night. We could have been murdered in our sleep."
> Ben: "Oh, come off it. Hardly anybody I know around here locks their windows at night, and we don't hear about murders going on."

> Kati: "Marlon, did you take my OverBank Visa? I can't find it."
> Marlon: "Of course I didn't take it. That's the third credit card you've lost in two months. You've got to be more careful or the crooks will find it and charge us into bankruptcy."
> Kati: "Well, we never did find that check you lost in the mountains — even after I told you to put it somewhere safe."
> Marlon: "I did put it somewhere safe."
> Kati: "The freezer is not a safe place for a check."
> Marlon: "Yes, it is. I read an article just the other day talking about that."
> Kati: "And every thief in the country now knows to check the freezer when burgling a house."

Do you see here that the subject of the lost credit card has been long ago abandoned and another subject has replaced it?

2. Exaggeration (hyperbole)
With this fallacy, an arguer exaggerates something to make the evidence or the argument itself appear more powerful and convincing.

> Amy: "Bill, what's wrong with you? You never help me clean up after a party. You always

> watch some mindless TV program and then fall asleep and snore loud enough to kill the fish in the lake outside."
>
> Bill: "Well, I don't help because you never ask me. I'm always ready to help."
>
> Amy: "Never asked you? That's the stupidest and lamest excuse I have ever heard in my whole life. Never asked you? I've asked you at least fourteen million times."

Exaggerating by using such terms as "you never," and "you always" is especially insulting.

3. Straw man

A straw man fallacy is constructed by an arguer in order to make winning — the point or the entire argument — easier. A straw man is created by describing an opponent's position in weak or obviously wrong, or exaggerated terms. This wildly exaggerated description is then simply brushed aside.

> Carl: "Before we close all the coal-fired and oil-fired power plants, we need to identify reliable alternatives."
>
> Mikey: "So what you're saying is that we should continue to let babies die from the toxic air pollution spewed out by the coal fired generation plants while we wait possibly decades for a 'reliable alternative' as you call it."

> Theo: "Ephesians 5:22 says that wives are to submit to their husbands.'
>
> Marla: "So what you're saying is that women are to be nothing but doormats, robots, slaves, Stepford wives, indentured servants,

> *menial, oppressed, subjugated lackeys to their husbands, who can order them to do anything they want."*

Notice that with this kind of response, Marla shows that she is not interested in learning or discussing what the Bible actually says about the relationship between husbands and wives. She is so repulsed by any idea of submission that she refuses to hear anything about it. Her wild exaggeration protects her from needing to think about it.

4. False analogy

Much of what we learn is achieved through the use of analogies: An unfamiliar thing or idea is compared with a familiar thing of idea, and the things they have in common or that are similar helps us understand the previously unfamiliar thing. For example:

An ordinary computer memory chip loses the information on it whenever the computer is turned off, because it needs electrical power to maintain it On the other hand, EPROM (Electrically Programmable Read Only Memory) works like a classroom marker board: When information is written on it, the information stays no matter how many times the computer power is turned on and off. The memory is erased, like the marker board, only when the user deliberately erases it.

Here, the working of an EPROM chip is made clearer by using a classroom marker board as an analogy.

However, in arguments or any type of persuasive discussion, a problem arises when the analogy is used *as if it were evidence for the argument rather than clarification* of how the argument works. Notice this false analogy:

> Dot: "Gray, I thought we agreed that you were going to stop wasting money by gambling it away."
> Gray: "Yes, Honey, and I am acting on that."
> Dot: "Then what's this letter from Apogee Investments, saying you gave them $3,000?"
> Gray: "That's an investment company. I got us into the stock market."
> Dot: "That's the same as throwing our money away. You buy some stocks and after a while the market goes down and takes the stocks and your money with it. It's pure gambling."

5. Red Herring

A red herring argument takes its name from fox hunting long ago. When the fox hunters on their horses and the hunting dogs began to close in on the fox during the chase, some of the hunting support staff would drag some pickled red herring fish across the path the fox had just taken. Because hunting dogs have exceptionally keen senses of smell, coming suddenly across the powerful odor of fish while their brains were amplifying the faint odor of the fox would throw the dogs off the scent and drive them in every direction.

So, red herring is the perfect name for the fallacy where one of the disputants, feeling that he or she is losing the argument, simply tosses in a red herring—changing the subject and taking the other person down a different line of thought.

> Kris: "Hans, why did you change our doctor from Dr. Bokrush to Dr. Kneedle?"
>
> Hans: "Dr. Kneedle has higher ratings. Look here on Whimper.com."
>
> Kris: "Don't you know you can't trust Whimpe.com? Look how well they rated Eatsumfat Donuts. And everyone knows what bad donuts they sell."
>
> Hans: "Their donuts are actually pretty good, I think."
>
> Kris: "Have you tried one of their BerryNut cupcakes? You could use one of them to play baseball with."

And so the couple is no longer discussing why Hans changed their doctor and instead are off on a red herring about a rating site.

6. Emotive Language

Some words have powerful emotional impacts, some good and some bad. Other words neutral or have their emotional appeal dependent on context. When words are used intentionally to influence the argument because of their emotional power, the fallacy of emotive language is committed.

> Lem: "How can you support Senator Crassie? He's a greedy exploiter who runs a "theft store" in skid row, where he steals money from the poor by overcharging them for junk merchandise."

> Lam: "Well, his opponent, who claims to be an advocate of the people, is for all intents and purposes a crook who sells his soul and his vote to the highest bidder. In other words, he's a political prostitute."
>
> Sally: "Fred, why haven't you mowed the lawn yet? Are you so immature that you can prefer your stupid train set over your obligations to the marriage?"
> Fred: "Well, I don't see you getting your fat rear end in gear to work on cleaning the living room of the junk you left after your so-called craft session. Looks to me like you're a lazy slug."

You can imagine how effective this interchange is for getting these tasks done and for strengthening the marriage.

7. ad hominem

An ad hominem ("to the man") argument leaves the subject of the dispute behind and instead attacks the person being argued with. It is easy to see how fallacious and unfair such a tactic is because a fact is a fact (as long as it is true) regardless of who offers it in an argument.

> Jill: "I don't see anything wrong if I call Mr. Thompson, our friendly neighbor, to find out the schedule he has programmed on his sprinkler timer."
> Mel: "I don't want you to do that. It looks bad."
> Jill: "I don't understand why it 'looks bad' as you say."

> Mel: "Everyone will think you're having an affair."
>
> Jill: "An affair? From a phone call? That's silly. I don't get that at all."
>
> Mel: "That's because you're stupid. If you can't see the obvious conclusion everyone will come to, then you must not have the mental capacity of a snail."

Obviously, stooping to a personal insult in any kind of discussion is offensive and illogical. Remember,

---

**The purpose of a discussion
or an argument is
to make a decision or solve a problem,
not to prove the other person wrong.**

✟

Appendix 10
Five Secret Keys to a Happy Marriage

1. From page 5

> **Secret Key #1 to a Happy Marriage**
> Never use a negative or sarcastic tone of voice.

2. From page 16

> **Secret Key #2 to a Happy Marriage**
> Make your every word and deed focus on making life for your spouse easier rather than more difficult.

3. From page 27

> **Secret Key #3 to a Happy Marriage**
> Always Remember Respect.
> Avoid sarcasm, insults, and condescension.

4. From page 47

> **Secret Key #4 to a Happy Marriage**
> Love is something you do
> Even more than something you feel.

5. From page 57

> **Secret Key #5 to a Happy Marriage**
> Use the Magic Words Frequently

✟

About the Author

Robert Harris was born in 1950 in Los Angeles, California. He holds a PhD in English from the University of California at Riverside.

Dr. Harris lives in Tustin with his excellent wife, Marie.

About the Cover

At some point in many marriages, what began as a peaceful gondola ride through the quiet canals of Venice turns into a wild, rough ride on a roller coaster, bouncing the spouses around and perhaps producing nausea. This book has been designed to prevent such queasiness or to point the way back to a smooth and happy relationshp.

Colophon

Proverbs are set in *Monotype Corsiva 14*
Comments are set in Book Antiqua 11
Study materials are set in Book Antiqua 10
Main Scripture passages in each chapter are set in *Georgia 11 italic*

www.ingramcontent.com/pod-product-compliance
Lightning Source LLC
Chambersburg PA
CBHW070547050426
42450CB00011B/2750